I LIKE THAT WORD

THE DAILY GRIPE STRIKES AGAIN

PeTRA — I hope
this causes uncontrolled
snorting.

Bob Eastley 10-29-19

eastleyr@ferris.edu
231-629-9106

Published by Seacoast Press, an imprint of MindStir Media, LLC
1931 Woodbury Ave. #182 | Portsmouth, New Hampshire 03801 | USA
1.800.767.0531 | www.seacoastpress.com

Printed in the United States of America
ISBN-13: 978-1-7329482-3-5

I LIKE THAT WORD

THE DAILY GRIPE STRIKES AGAIN

BY ROBERT EASTLEY

SEACOAST

PRESS

DEDICATION

Special thanks to all my family and friends, especially Amy and Sarah, and my wife, Jan. Her way with words and suggestions are woven into many of these stories. I'd like to dedicate this book to three people. The first is my brother, Mark, who fought so hard and lost his battle with cancer. I miss you, buddy. The other two are Jack and Alex, who've stolen my heart.

CONTENTS

CHAPTER 1

KIDS AND OTHER AWKWARD CREATURES

GABRIEL, BLOW YOUR TRUMPET

December 21 is approaching, and with it the alleged impending end of the world, according to the Mayan Calendar and a number of quirky celebrities. If they're right, you may wish to rethink your Christmas shopping strategy. You could be really extravagant and buy lavish gifts for everyone, just assuming that the credit card bill will never arrive, but what if the Mayans were wrong? Maybe your best bet is to just put everything on layaway.

It occurred to me that, if the Mayans were right, we'd be ringside for the big blast from Gabriel's trumpet announcing Judgment Day. And that got me thinking that I used to own a trumpet, or actually its twin sister, the cornet.

My parents were wonderful people, usually logical and pragmatic. I have no idea what possessed them to buy me a horn and then expect me to actually learn to play it. It was dreadful. Actually, I was dreadful. To say the least, no one ever mistook me for Satchmo or Gabriel or even the guy occupying third chair in the junior high band. I sounded more like a flock of demented geese.

Anyhow, I was issued the stupid thing, and it was made clear to me that, now that we owned it, I was going to by-gosh learn to play it. Did I mention that I was awful? I sat in my room with the door closed, trying to decipher what those notes on the music sheet meant, oblivious to the difference between flats, sharps, and Shinola. I practiced an excruciating (I like that word) hour a day, belting out random notes like B and G and S and Q with no sense of rhythm whatsoever.

However, what I lacked in skill, I more than made up for in volume. The thing was disturbingly loud, much to the dismay of both my folks and the neighbors on either side of our house. If you wonder why parents sometimes seem a little tense, it may be because they just came home from a bad day at work, and now their home, their sanctuary, is filled with the noise of a brass bazooka being massacred by an unlicensed operator.

At some point, I graduated from my bedroom to dead-last chair in the junior high band. There were boys and girls in the first and second chairs who could actually read music and play the school fight song or something from John Philip Sousa. I was in last chair, located on the east side of the parking lot, hanging out with all the other last-chair rejects and reading *Mad Magazine.*

So, after school, we'd all stay for band practice, and some poor soul who had drawn the short straw tried to prepare us to actually play music. Quadratic equations? Easy. Herding cats? Kid's stuff. Try to make them sit still and play coordinated sheet music.

Finally, after months of pointless practice, I reached the culmination of my musical career. We were the featured act in a band concert for all our family and friends. What's worse than horrible? All the top chair people were up there playing beautifully. Unfortunately, nobody heard them. They were being sabotaged and drowned out by the rest of us who were belting out a catastrophic cacophony of uncoordinated crap.

The audience was a vision of shock and terror. Moms were trying to smile, but they were grimacing. Children were crying. Grandparents were turning off their hearing aids. Dads were looking at their watches and hoping to get back in time for the second half. Yes, it was that bad.

A little word of advice: If you plan to buy your child a musical instrument, consider something that's fairly low on the decibel scale. And, if possible, select something that they can use for a lifetime. You know, like a radio.

ROCKET FOOTBALL: STARS OF THE FUTURE

Recently I was whisked back on a magic carpet of memories to those thrilling days of yesteryear, as I was in attendance at a local Rocket football game. Those were some of the happiest days of my life, a time when I couldn't wait for Saturday morning and the big game.

First, there were the uniforms. The helmet, shoulder pads, and jersey were all fine, but the coolest things were the pants. They were two-toned and stretchy and had an inside pocket where you could insert those thigh pads with the big ridges on them. When I had those on, I was unstoppable. I could run like the wind, stiff-arming would-be tacklers, and dancing through a defense like Paul Hornung. Knute Rockne would have been proud. My friends and family were thrilled. Pro scouts followed my every move. Of course, it's been a long time. JFK was president then, and I was only nine. I suppose it's possible that my memories are slightly distorted . . .

In truth, it was really fun to be a fly on the wall, er, in the bleachers, and take in all the proceedings at our local game. First, there were the players themselves. The range of talent and understanding is pretty wide at the eight and nine-year-old level. On the one hand, there's a quarterback with good hands, great speed, and the ability to run, pass, keep track of twenty or more plays, and get his whole gaggle organized on the field. The first string looks like a well-oiled machine and likely has less "illegal procedure" infractions than our local NFL team. At the other end of the spectrum is a skinny little forty-pound kid, with a uniform that hangs off him like a pup tent, who's either feeding popcorn to the birds or lying on his back and eating peanut butter and jelly, absolutely oblivious to whatever's happening on the field. I saw one kid with an electronic Gameboy, another throwing a soggy pair of socks back and forth with a kid in the stands, and two other guys thumping each other on the helmet, apparently seeing how far you could go before it hurt.

At this level, the punt is a free kick, so all the players kneel down, and the punter sends it into orbit. Or, as in this case, the punter hammered a line-drive directly into the back of his teammate's head from a range of six feet (which is why they wear helmets). The ball may also go straight up or possibly even backward, but that just adds to the fun.

The rule in Rocket football is that everybody has to play. So, at some point in the game, the little guy with the PB&J is called forth from wherever he's been picking daisies, and they throw him in at right tackle. I saw one cute little boy get tossed into the fray in the fourth quarter, and they lined him up across from some monster of a kid who was probably already shaving. Picture Dick Butkus matched up with Martin Short, and you get my drift. The little kid with the skinny legs got into a three-point stance, with his rear end almost on the ground, so he looked just like a frog. The ball was snapped, and the big bully launched out and absolutely plastered him. The kid tried to get up, and Dick pulverized him again. Unfortunately, Martin's team got a first down, so the poor little tyke was pancaked on seven straight plays. Finally, they punted, and he came out, found the remains of his sandwich, and went back to feeding bread crusts to the birds.

The other really fun thing to watch is the parents. Most are there cheering and supporting just like they should be, but there's always one father, probably a frustrated ex-wannabe football hero, who is living vicariously through his son. He's there to see his kid put a big hurt on somebody. In our case, it was a dad from the visiting team who looked as though he may have been recently paroled. He was about six feet tall, conservatively two hundred and sixty pounds, with a shaved head, copious tattoos, and arms the size of power poles. He spent the entire game screaming at the top of his lungs, encouraging Trevor to do a Ray Nitschke and hammer somebody. "C'mon, defense. Let's kill 'em. C'mon Trevor, take his head off . . ." I watched as Trevor came off the field. He didn't look anything like his dad, and nothing at all like Ray Nitschke. In fact, he looked more like the kid from *Home Alone*. Poor Trevor. I'm afraid he may grow up with issues. But on this day, he went and found his bologna sandwich and sprawled out on his back to look at the clouds.

THE CAMPING TRIP

It's been a long time since I was in Scouts, but I remember my first real overnight camping trip with an eerie clarity. I suppose trauma has that sort of impact on one's gray matter. The whole thing sounded so fun. Our troop leader had us all over to his house for a planning meeting to decide what food, clothing, equipment, weapons, etc. we needed to take. We, of course, figured he was a modern-day reincarnation of Daniel Boone or Jeremiah Johnson, one of a mere handful of men privy to the hidden secrets of the forest. In retrospect, he was more of a Ward Cleaver. His idea of a wilderness experience was loosening his tie to mow the lawn.

Anyhow, we had an early morning rendezvous in some parking lot and then headed for the drop zone in a caravan of old station wagons. After what seemed like hours of driving, we finally stopped and unloaded our gear where a dirt road intersected a two-track. The plan was to set a course and schlep our stuff a mile or more back to the campsite. This presented a problem on several levels. First, Jeremiah forgot his compass and didn't know south from Shinola. Plus, he couldn't remember which side of the tree the moss grows on, so we wandered around like a lost tribe in the wilderness for the better part of the morning.

This wouldn't have been so bad, but there was a great disparity in the amount of gear being portaged by various members of the lost boys. In retrospect, this being a one-night expedition, I'd have been fine with a sweatshirt, a sleeping bag, and a couple peanut butter sandwiches. However, several mothers weren't ABOUT to let their sons go off into the great unknown without adequate clothing and provisions. We all had those olive-green backpacks stuffed full of mess kits, canteens, knives, ropes, flashlights, towels, pillows, slingshots, comic books, six complete changes of clothes and enough food (each) to supply an Everest expedition for three months (Sherpas included). One kid, in addition to this, had a SUITCASE, one of those big beasts that held enough clothing for a trip to Europe. In short, we were a bunch of sixty-pound kids carrying around seventy pounds of stuff.

Finally, after three or four hours of steady hiking, each of us sweaty, grimy and exhausted, our faithful guide finally stumbled into a small clearing and decided that this was home. Unfortunately, it was surrounded on three sides by a massive swamp (and all the hungry critters that reside therein). The first order of business was to set up our pup tents and then begin foraging for firewood. Did I mention that we were in a swamp? The first order of business SHOULD have been to fly in a crop duster and spray the entire area with industrial-strength DEET. It's difficult to concentrate on tent stakes with a few thousand deer flies and mosquitoes trying to extract a unit of blood, but we finally managed and crawled inside. That's when we discovered the truth about canvas pup tents. They aren't waterproof, windproof, or bug proof. All they really provide is a place to change your underwear in private.

Once the wood was collected, our fearless leader attempted to light a fire with two sticks and a piece of twine. Right. When that failed, he dumped the contents of his cigarette lighter on the kindling and used a match. While this was going on, several of us were instructed to find a suitable site and dig a latrine. Let me tell you about ten-year-old boys. They're the most self-conscious people on the planet, and not

ABOUT to make a deposit in a public hole-in-the-ground that the other guys might witness and tease them about. Needless to say, we all found our own trees, and the latrine was the cleanest place in the camp.

Finally, as darkness fell over this merry band, we tried valiantly to cook dinner over an open fire. I recall a semi-delicious blend of mostly raw potatoes and partially cooked greasy hamburger mixed with some pork and beans. Luckily, somebody brought marshmallows. Finally, after a few rousing choruses of "99 Bottles of Beer on the Wall," we crawled into our low-tech sleeping bags to escape the mosquitoes and read *Superman* by flashlight. And, sometime after midnight, we were treated to one of those special thunderstorms that brings to mind a cow whizzing on a flat rock. It took about twenty minutes for the water to start seeping through the tent from above and the sleeping bag from below. Well, as my wife's Uncle Web profoundly said, you can only get so wet, and then it runs off.

THE GREAT FISHING EXCURSION

I have fishing genes. Not the "J" type that bunch up in the legs of your waders, but the ones that make it difficult to focus on mowing the lawn. They certainly aren't the recessive variety. I got a double whammy from my dad on one side and my maternal grandfather on the other. Luckily, my passion was shared by my first cousins, Jim and Kup, so growing up was a fish-fest.

Dad was a good bass and pike fisherman, and very proficient at dropping a Mepps spinner into tight spots while stream fishing for trout. My grandfather gave us our first taste of fly-fishing. When I was a kid, Dad, Grandpa, and an occasional uncle would hit the Pere Marquette or the Pine or some local creek to catch enough trout for breakfast the next morning. You can keep your prime rib. If you've never had a creel full of brook trout fried in bacon grease, along with toast, juice, and a big pile of fried potatoes, put it on your bucket list.

Like all kids, I just had to pester. Every time they headed out on one of these adventures, I begged to go along. Every time it was the same response. Wait 'till you're a little older. Fishing for bluegills off the dock was one thing. Stream fishing was a bit more complicated.

Well, one day, out of the blue, it happened. I got the nod. I felt like a relief pitcher going in for his first big league appearance. Bring in the right-handed seven-year-old. They were going to try a little "crik" north of town, and this one was small and shallow enough that I probably wouldn't fall in and drown. I hardly slept. At four in the morning, I was up sorting through my inventory, making sure I had enough hooks and sinkers, checking my reel, and waiting for the stupid sun to come up.

Dad, Grandpa, and I had breakfast and headed out, getting to the stream at about eight. It was a gorgeous day, chilly, sunny, a few mosquitoes looking for a snack, and the promise of fish. Dad headed upstream in waders, deftly throwing spinners as he went. Gramp was in old boots and planned to creep downstream, drifting worms into the lairs of some unsuspecting trout. I also had a worm rod. He planted me at the downstream end of a big culvert where the creek flowed into a nice hole. Then he explained, in words I could understand, that great rewards come to those who are diligent. He headed off, saying he'd be back in about an hour.

I had the attention span of a puppy. I dunked worms for about four and a half minutes and then started getting antsy, sure that I was missing out on something. I decided to abandon the mission and go find gramps. Picture a four-foot kid carrying a six-foot rod with eight feet of monofilament through ten-foot brambles. I fell in the mud, tore my shirt, got my line hopelessly snarled, and was a complete mess by the time I finally found him.

He said he'd be happy to trade, so he went and sat by that culvert, and I wandered downstream, dropping my line into any hole with enough water to float a worm. I stuck with it for forty-five minutes, making just enough noise to scare every living creature within a half mile. And then, with a heavy heart and a not-so-heavy creel, I headed back to the culvert.

Some lessons are learned in school. Others are only available in the classroom of life. I found out a little something about patience that day. When I returned, a disheveled mud, bug and mono magnet, my grandfather just smiled and asked how I'd done. I looked at the ground and mumbled something about them not biting. So, he opened up that old wicker creel and showed me the finest limit of gorgeous 10-12 inch rainbows and brook trout you've ever seen. He'd even thrown back some smaller ones.

I tried to be happy for him, but I'm sure I looked pretty pouty and low. He wasn't worried. He told me there'd be plenty of other days. As usual, he was right.

THE PRIZE

When I was a little shaver, my parents used to hang out with two very dear friends. We'll call them, let's see, Rob and Laura, Ward and June, Lester and Earl (oops, never mind), I know, Char and Hap. Anyhow, they were the world's nicest people, like everyone's favorite aunt and uncle. They didn't have any kids of their own, so basically made a big fuss over my brother and me, gave us cool stuff, and spoiled us rotten. Even if Char got all mushy and told us how much we'd grown and how handsome we were, that was okay, because she was such a nice lady.

One weekend, we all went down to visit them, and Hap decided to spice things up a bit for the younger generation. He announced that we were going to have a contest, a decathlon of sorts, with a mixture of events, pitting my skills as a warrior against my kid brother's. The declared winner, the champion of champions, was to be awarded THE

PRIZE, something so amazing and incredible that its identity couldn't be divulged until after the contest was completed.

I have to tell you that my mind was swimming in a sea of anticipation. The possibilities were simply endless. Was it an official NFL football? A new baseball glove? Maybe one of those BB guns that you could actually pump up to higher pressure? How about a slot car set? I'm telling you, it was like finding out that Santa had found a stash of lost presents, and was planning a surprise second visit in July.

I don't remember too much about the contest itself, but I recall it being the kinds of things anyone might set up in the backyard. So, we had to long jump over a flower bed and high jump over a bamboo pole and race across the yard and throw a baseball as far as we could . . . and other manly tests of skill and daring.

It was all I could do to focus on the task at hand because my mind kept conjuring up endless possibilities of what grand thing awaited the winner. Was it a mask and flippers like Lloyd Bridges wore on *Sea Hunt*? Maybe a fiberglass fishing rod with one of those open-face reels?

As the morning grew warmer and stickier, we finally completed the last event. With a three-year advantage over my brother Mark (pretty significant at eight or nine), the result was never really in doubt, but the taste of victory was still very sweet. We came into the house, only to discover that we all had to sit down to soup and sandwiches, and the award ceremony would follow lunch. The anticipation was killing me, and it was all I could do to sit still and be polite while my parents and our hosts SLOWLY sipped their coffee and chatted about boring grown-up stuff.

Finally, with the dessert finished and the dishes rinsed, Hap announced that it was time to crown the victor and (at long last) disclose the nature of the prize. I was told to shut my eyes, but in my mind, I was picturing a pair of those rubber hip boots for wading in the creek, or perhaps a Schwinn bike with the three-speed shifter on the handlebars, or maybe even a new puppy.

It was time, and I opened my eyes. I was scarcely prepared for the sight that greeted me. There, in all its glory, was the culmination of all my dreams and efforts. It was a genuine vinyl, chocolate brown, zipper-up-the-middle, no kid should be without one . . . shaving bag. I was speechless. I should mention that, at the time of this contest, I was almost a decade away from having peach fuzz on my chin, and my blonde hair was buzzed to about a sixteenth of an inch over my entire head, so I had no need of a brush. I was way too young to be using cologne or deodorant, so I'd just been issued a full-sized shaving kit to hold my ONLY personal hygiene possession, a toothbrush.

The hard part was sitting there, all eyes upon me, Hap grinning proudly from ear to ear, and me trying to look excited about my great fortune. I felt like I was gut-shot. Yes, I know, I should have been grateful, but I was as self-centered as any kid that age and feeling sorry for myself. I'm sure I mumbled a half-hearted thank you and made a complete fool of myself.

So, since it's the holiday season, here's a word to the wise for anyone about to start Christmas shopping for a young son: If he can't ride it, throw it, or shoot it, you might want to consider Plan B.

ALL ABOUT EDUCATED DRIVERS

There's nothing more exciting for a teenager who's pushing sixteen (or more frightening to his/her parents) than the prospect of getting his driver's license. Things have changed a bit since I was learning to operate a motor vehicle. Nowadays, Mom and Dad have to privately contract with someone brave enough to spend time in traffic with a complete novice. Back in my day, the school provided a vehicle and some poor teacher who had drawn the short straw and had his life insurance paid up.

In our car, we had Clyde. He was riding herd over me, some poor little girl who had absolutely no affinity for operating mechanical equipment, and some mouthy jock who was pretty sure he knew it all. For him, driving lessons were just a waste of time.

This group met before school every day for what seemed like months. We'd arrive groggy and grouchy in the pitch dark, and each would take a turn behind the wheel doing whatever task was appropriate for the day. At the age of fifteen, I would have enjoyed some Beatles or Tommy James on the radio to keep us company, but Clyde had other ideas. First, he was a little hard of hearing, and he was also a big fan of really hick country music, which blared at all times at a decibel level that could have melted steel. It was swell.

In theory, all three students in the car had to learn all the nuances (I like that word) of driving in a few short days, and Clyde was there to apply the brakes or fix any dilemma that we created for ourselves. I say "in theory," because he was the type to let us learn from our mistakes, and was more of a spectator than a participant.

I don't recall being particularly poor at any specific aspect of driving. My only hindrance was that I was about five-foot-nothing and could barely see over the wheel, a fact that jock-boy enjoyed pointing out on a daily basis. However, I did discover that I'm a really lousy passenger, and I become, shall we say, rather anxious when an idiot is behind the wheel.

I remember two days in vivid detail. The first was when Clyde decided that the little twerp of a girl should try to parallel park in the middle of downtown just when the traffic was beginning to ramp up. She was petrified. Clyde was cool. He had Faron Young on the radio singing loudly enough to drown out a jackhammer. This freaked the girl out even worse. So, she pulled in wrong, and pulled back out . . . HELLO WALLS . . . tried again, and it was worse . . . BUT LONELY WALLS, I'LL KEEP YOU COMPANY . . . By now, there were six cars stacked up behind us. She started making little whimpering noises and pulled in again . . . HELLO CEILING. I'M GONNA STARE AT YOU A WHILE . . . this time making contact with the car in front and pulled back out. Now there were twelve cars, and they were honking. She was sobbing. Clyde was fine.

The other day worthy of mention was when Clyde had us doing some country driving. This time, Big Shot was behind the wheel. We came to a stop sign at a major highway crossing. Nothing on the right. Just a semi bearing down on the left. Junior looked both ways and simply pulled out. As the guy in the left side passenger seat, I was going to die first, but only by milliseconds. The truck driver had panic in his eyes, and my entire, fairly short, and boring life flashed in front of me. Luckily, the idiot gunned it, and the big rig missed turning us into a greasy spot by about a car width. Even Clyde wasn't smiling. The kid said, "I thought it was a four-way stop."

The only good thing about the whole situation was that jock jerk never uttered another sarcastic word for the rest of the lessons. I'm no worse for wear, either, although, if a Faron Young song comes on the radio, I break out in a cold sweat.

A DAY AT MUSCLE BEACH

Looking out the window on this April morning, there's about a half inch of new sneet (a sloppy sleet/snow surprise) on the ground, and absolutely nothing to hint that the summer season is lurking in the shadows. However, Memorial Day is next month, and with it the alleged kickoff to some warmer weather, so I'm trying to have faith that things will change for the better.

As a high school punk, one of my favorite summer vacation pastimes was going to the beach at Holland or Grand Haven on Lake Michigan. One of my friends had an old beater Chevy with rusty bumpers and three on the column. It wasn't much to look at, but it was a by-gosh convertible, and custom-made for three or four worldly high school boys who wanted to go cruisin' and make the summer scene.

One of the other guys even had a real surfboard, and we'd make a weekend of it, sleeping on the beach, listening to WLS on the transistor radio, body and board surfing, soaking up some rays, and (of course) checking out the exotic girls as they strolled up the beach. Note that, to be exotic, you only had to be from some other high school.

I vividly recall one hot, sunny afternoon, walking up the beach, a bronze-skinned Adonis with muscles rippling and hair flowing in the offshore breeze. Men admired and tried to emulate me. Women secretly longed for me. If I'd had a role in *Beach Blanket Bingo*, I'm quite sure that Annette Funicello would have dumped Frankie like a plate of moldy leftovers.

Anyway, as I strolled through the surf, a vision of strength and grace, a beautiful blonde girl rushed up to me and said, "Hey . . . HEY, stupid . . . you're getting sunburned." Huh? Nuts, it was all a dream. The girl vaporized and left me with nothing but a good case of lobster skin and my friend Dave kicking sand on me to wake me up.

Okay, the Adonis thing may have been a bit of a stretch. A protestant Woody Allen might have been closer. At 5'-4" and 122 pounds, sporting a Princeton haircut and the latest in brown, plastic glasses, and rounding out the ensemble with just a hint of peach fuzz on my upper lip, I was all but invisible to members of the opposite sex. All I needed was a swimsuit with a pocket protector, and I could have passed for a sixteen-year-old Bill Gates.

Ah, but all that didn't matter. The waves were wonderful, and the hotdogs we cooked on the beach tasted like prime rib. We'd swim all day until we were as waterlogged as an old sofa left on the curb, and then build a fire on the beach until we finally crashed.

Sometimes, pods of girls would happen by and talk to us. A couple of my friends had sideburns and could pass for twenty, so they got noticed. They'd tell lies about being all-conference in some sport and owning their own muscle cars and dating college girls. They were just white lies. I stayed in the background, looking like somebody's kid brother, so summer romance was a distant dream, but so what? On Sunday evening, we'd head home to the drudgery of living with our parents and working our summer jobs. Luckily, the weekend was only five days away.

THE PROM: THEN AND NOW

There is an event out there on the horizon that strikes fear into the hearts of most normal adults. You might think that it's menopause, or perhaps a visit to the proctologist, or even the threat of nuclear devastation. However, as the calendar rolls into May, nothing raises our blood pressures like the impending high school senior prom.

I remember the prom. At least, I have a distant, somewhat naïve memory of how they used to be. The prom was a formal dance. Either the girl borrowed a dress from her older sister, or her mom spent a couple of weeks feverishly sewing and hemming and creating a homemade work of art. The boys pulled a gray suit out of the closet and brushed off a quarter inch of dust that had been accumulating on the shoulders since their grandparents' fiftieth anniversary.

Mom spent all afternoon curling her daughter's hair, and the guys went all out, not only showering but scraping the fuzz off their chins and upper lips. They picked up their dates in Dad's station wagon, went to dinner in a local restaurant that didn't require you to clear your own table, and arrived promptly at eight for the start of the dance.

Once it got into full swing, the chaperones were kept fairly busy. They had to keep an eagle eye on the punch bowl, just in case some kid tried to spice it up with a pint of hooch. Plus, they frequently had to tell different couples to stop groping and leave a little air space between their teenage parts, but the whole thing was pretty tame. Finally, after dancing until midnight, everyone headed for the local hamburger joint and got home by the one a.m. curfew.

Things have changed. First, a young lady will now spend two months and about $500 in gas money to scour the countryside in search of the perfect dress. It will cost more than your first car. These dresses are disposable. They may only be worn once. It is absolutely unacceptable to borrow one from an older sister or one of her friends, as someone may recognize it as having been previously occupied.

Next, the young woman will need copious cosmetic procedures. These will include hair extensions, coloring, curling, clipping, and highlighting, as well as manicures, pedicures, and other cures that I can't even begin to remember. Said procedures will require a specialized team of hairdressers and groomers working uninterrupted for eight straight hours. She will be transformed into a thing of beauty. Oh, by the way, this will cost more than your second car.

Your daughter will be picked up by her date at seven. He will be wearing a rented tuxedo and driving a rented Mustang or Camaro that has ten or twelve cylinders and can go from zero to 120 in the time it takes you to sneeze. Unfortunately, there is no suitable cuisine within a hundred-mile radius, so they'll be dining in an intimate little restaurant located 142 miles away on the Lake Michigan shoreline. This means that, by the time they drive across the state (the long way), eat dinner, and return, they will be arriving at the prom about thirty minutes before it's over.

After two dances, they'll rush home, change into casual attire, and begin the second phase of the evening, which consists of rendezvousing with forty or fifty of their counterparts at someone's friend's cousin's uncle's cottage about thirty miles from town. They'll want to stay there all night and then return to town for a late breakfast.

This plan may cause you some alarm, and while anguishing about such things as alcohol and your daughter's virtue, you'll suggest that nothing good ever happens after midnight. However, there is absolutely nothing to worry about. Why, you ask? Well, luckily, one of the cousin's friend's uncle's half-nephews, a twenty-two-year-old parolee with multiple body piercings and a valid ID, will be there to chaperone. You see? And you were worried.

And so, at approximately ten the following morning, you can expect them to return home, a little exhausted and disheveled, but brimming with wonderful tales of the previous night's adventures. Some may even be based on a true story.

LEAVE IT TO THEODORE

It was a stark, gloomy November afternoon in 1970. The leaves had long since fallen, and there was a hint of snow in the air. Just before four o'clock, approximately thirty young men made their way into the dark recesses of Douglass Houghton Hall on the Michigan Tech campus. What was their mission? Were they some sort of cult? Perhaps a northern chapter of the SDS, intent on protesting the Vietnam War or initiating some radical action against the university's administration? Were they plotting to take over the cafeteria and lay waste to the remaining seventy-five pounds of eight-day-old Jell-O? Ah, very plausible theories, all of these, but incorrect. These boys weren't into mischief. They were just taking a break from their studies to watch *Leave it to Beaver*.

1970 was a simpler time. There were no cell phones or Internet, and tablets were something hauled down by Moses from Mount Sinai. Dorm rooms were also a bit less luxurious than they are now. There were two desks, four walls, and two bunk beds, which were the perfect place to stockpile your laundry until you took it home for your mom to wash at Thanksgiving. There was just one communal shower area and bathroom. It didn't pay to be shy.

In fact, the whole place had a military feel to it. Nobody had a TV in the room, so we all paraded downstairs to watch the one-and-only television in a dingy alcove affectionately referred to as "The Dungeon." And the one program we never missed was *Leave it to Beaver*.

What a classic show. I bring it up now because I recently rediscovered it on cable. I'm not sure why we all loved it so much. Maybe it was because Wally and Beaver were about our age. Maybe it was because we all knew a smooth-talking operator like Eddie Haskell or a big, clumsy doofus like Lumpy Rutherford. Likely, most of us in the Boomer generation had no-nonsense dads who worked hard all day and wanted to come home to dinner and the newspaper, just like Ward Cleaver. Ward, like our dads, expected the lawn to be mowed when he got home, and the kids kept quiet and watched their table manners at dinner. Shut up and eat your broccoli.

Mostly, it was because the plot of every *Leave it to Beaver* episode was a slice of real life. Beaver lost his milk money seven days in a row and didn't know what to do. Eddie talked Wally into taking the shortcut in his dad's car and ended up stranded in the boondocks after running through a massive puddle. Beaver found a lost dog and smuggled him into the house. Nobody was on drugs. No one's girlfriend was pregnant. You could ride around with six guys hanging out of an old jalopy, and nobody cared. There was such simplicity.

Also, and maybe this is what sets it apart from so many of today's idiotcoms, the adult head of the household wasn't some forty-year-old adolescent with the IQ of cottage cheese. He was tough. He was a role model. He was in charge. He was even kinda scary. Mom was the rock they could count on. She made their lunches and sent them off to school. She had cake and milk waiting for them when they got home. Maybe I just miss being a kid. Hey, Wally?

CHAPTER 2

FOOD FOR THOUGHT

THE EARL OF HAMBURGER

There's long been a controversy about who first summited Mt. Everest. Sir Edmund Hillary generally gets credit for making the climb in 1953. There's also a fair chance that Andrew (Sandy) Irvine beat him to it by almost thirty years, but the fact that he's still up there somewhere clouds the issue a bit. In my opinion, Tenzing Norgay, a Sherpa (that's Nepalese for caddy), should get the lion's (or in this case the yeti's) share of the credit. He not only climbed the mountain, but he schlepped Ed's food, clothing, camping equipment, comic books, golf clubs, and other stuff up there in the process. Now there's your real mountaineer.

Likewise, there's some disagreement about who invented the sandwich. Rabbi Hillel the Elder (they shouldn't make fun of a guy's age) apparently put lamb, nuts, and veggies between two slices of unleavened bread during Passover back in the first century B.C.

However, much like Ed Hillary, credit for the invention goes to John Montagu, the 4th Earl of Sandwich, who was winning at the craps table back in 1762. He was on a hot streak, so he slapped some mutton and vegetables between two slices of bread and kept playing. Hold the mayo. Interestingly, Montagu was almost named the Earl of Portsmouth. I'll have a salami portsmouth on rye, please.

So much for your history lesson. The point of this story is that Big John wanted to turn supper into finger food. The bread let him hold it in one hand while he threw dice with the other.

Fast forward to the present day. We're at war. No, I'm not talking about whose nuclear button is bigger. I'm talking hamburger wars. Let's start with fast food. According to the Internet (which is always accurate), you can get a Quad Baconator at Wendy's or a Triple Whopper at Burger King. That's a big chunk of meat, not to mention some serious fat grams. Well, it's only a matter of time before some rocket surgeon discovers how to stack six or even seven patties onto one bun. The Behemoth Burger.

Meanwhile, the independents are also getting in on the action. I've heard tales of things you'd only dare whisper about; a monstrosity with two full pounds of ground beef, a layer of ham, a fried egg, ten strips of bacon, onion rings, barbeque sauce, and three kinds of cheese on a mutant ciabatta roll. Order it with a Diet Coke and a side of Plavix.

Do you see what's happening? We need to stop this madness. Bigger doesn't mean better. That's true for dry flies, and it goes for hamburgers, as well. If you had the time and utensils, wouldn't you prefer a twenty-ounce T-bone? A hamburger is a just a portable steak substitute. Portable. It was invented so you could eat with one hand while steering through rush hour traffic with the other.

Meanwhile, whenever I'm trying to chow down a cheeseburger while driving, it seems like a big glop of that ketchup/mustard/mayo/grease mixture invariably lands on my khakis. Dang. Your challenge is to invent some sort of edible burger-carrying unit that's drip-free and designed to protect your clothing. If you're successful, we'll dub thee The Earl of Hamburger.

CAFETERIA PROTOCOL

Although I infrequently frequent these establishments, I recently found myself dining in a cafeteria. It's not a restaurant. It's an assembly line where you step/slide, point to an item, put it on your tray, step/slide and point again until you hit the cash register. When properly done, it resembles a well-choreographed dance routine.

This particular venue was pretty uncomplicated. All they had were hot dogs, a variety of deli sandwiches, soups, prepackaged salads, and sandwich toppings. That's it. Everything was listed on the wall and staring at you as you slid along. Just point and shuffle.

Unfortunately, I found myself behind Marge and Jerry, a middle-aged couple, who, if they moved in next door, would cause you to move to another town, possibly Reykjavik. Jerry was an ultra-nervous control freak (I gleaned this in ninety seconds of observation). He kept pacing back and forth from where Marge was trying to order, up to the cashier to ask stupid questions about whether drinks were included, then back to Marge, then back to the cashier to ask if they used mayonnaise or Miracle Whip and blah, blah, blah. It was like watching a tiger in a cage.

Finally, he settled back in line next to Marge, a woman with a brain made of oatmeal, likely a result of years spent in close proximity to Jerry. The place has ham, turkey, Italian, tuna, and chicken salad. That's all. It's on the board. Marge asked if they had egg salad. The worker replied, "No, ma'am. Just what's on the board."

Jerry piped in with, "What kind of soup do you have?"

The woman replied, "Chili and chicken noodle." Both were listed on the Daily Special placard that was eighteen inches from his face.

He asked if they could get chicken noodle in a bread bowl, and when she said they could, he replied, "Fine, we'll have that."

While the worker got the soup, Jerry hovered over Marge and kept

29

muttering in her ear. She looked haggard. Finally, both bread bowls arrived, and he said, "Oh, no. We only wanted one. I'm having a sandwich."

Marge looked puzzled and asked, "Then who's the soup for?"

Jerry replied, "Well, honey, I knew you liked chicken soup, so I just assumed you'd have it."

Anyhow, while I stood in line, these nitwits sent both soups back and started over. The woman behind the counter was getting visibly perturbed (I like that word), and the line was getting longer. Finally, Marge ordered an Italian sandwich on rye, and Jerry jumped right in. "Well, honey, you know salami doesn't always agree with you. How about turkey?" She said no, but he was relentless. "Well, if you get turkey, we could split it and get a salad, but I'd rather have white bread."

By now, I'd been enjoying this little snapshot of wedded bliss for about ten minutes, and the worker was rolling her eyes at me. Finally, Marge hit her boiling point. She gave Jerry a look that suggested he might soon be seeking alternative living arrangements, and said, quite loudly, "I'll HAVE the Italian on rye."

Some people are just clueless, and Jerry opened his mouth once more to offer some useful tidbit but was cut short when the guy behind me started clapping. He actually started clapping. The worker started smirking, and Jerry got all flushed and actually ordered his own sandwich. And, it should have ended there, but they still hadn't checked out, now had they?

As it turns out, Marge is the keeper of the royal cash and has it stashed somewhere in the bowels (I don't like that word) of a monstrous purse large enough to hold your gear for a two-week backpacking trip to Yellowstone. She got to the register and started rummaging, pulling out combs, snot rags, mirrors, makeup, car keys and spare tires, and all the while telling the cashier her life story, the ages and locations of all her children and grandchildren, and what they had for dinner last night. I found it quite fascinating.

I looked back at the woman behind the counter, gave her a small wink, and asked, "Say, do you have hamburgers?"

FAST FOOD: THE EARLY YEARS

My good friend Tim used to be a bartender at Schuberg's. This was in the good old days when (as he put it) there weren't any pinheads cluttering up the place. There also weren't any pink drinks or blue drinks or low-carb drinks or cute little umbrellas. Nobody left a tip. You bellied up to the bar for a shot and a chaser and then stumbled home for pot roast.

In similar fashion, the early days of fast food restaurants were fairly basic. They had hamburgers and fries . . . period. There were no special orders. The burgers came with mustard, ketchup, onions, and pickles, and if you didn't like it, you picked it off. They also didn't have a numbering system. You couldn't order a #5 combo, because all they had was a #1 combo, so there really wasn't much point in numbering it.

And then, things changed. People stopped smoking and started jogging. At some point, health food and nutrition became the buzzwords, so foods high in calories and fat grams were taboo. So, reluctantly, the burger joints were forced to expand their menus to compete with the family restaurants.

First, they had to create new sandwiches, something that would leave you drooling like Pavlov's Pomeranian at the mere mention of chicken or fish with special toppings. I loved the media blitz that always preceded a new product line. Six weeks before a new sandwich hit the menu, they'd saturate the airwaves with, "Coming soon, for a limited time only, the Double Fish Sandwich." So, what was that all about? Were they patiently waiting for special instructions from headquarters describing how to stack two patties onto one bun? And, at some point in the future, would the technique no longer be feasible, and they'd have to scrap the mission? I used to work in a pretty popular family restaurant. If you wanted a hamburger with coleslaw and grape jelly on it, I could build one for you. Not on the menu? Just ask.

Then came the next earth-shattering idea . . . salads. They were pre-made and stored in those convenient plastic containers with the nifty lids that you couldn't remove without a crowbar and a graduate degree in mechanical engineering. Then, assuming you got it open, you had to try to consume the contents with the standard issue light-gauge plastic fork that snapped the first time you speared a cucumber slice.

The most entertaining part was watching the customer try to deal with the Dreaded Tomato Wedge. Those salads always seemed to come with a monstrous slice of tomato about the size of a tennis ball, and the poor slob trying to eat it had nothing but the previously mentioned fork. Hmmm . . . what to do? Method 1 was to stab the wedge and nibble at it a little at a time, sort of like eating a corn dog. Method 2 was attempting to cut the wedge with the side of the fork, which normally resulted in either mashing the tomato or catapulting it across the aisle into someone's lap. Method 3, my personal favorite, was when the patron put the entire wedge into his mouth, and then tried to look casual. This specialized procedure actually required you to disconnect your jawbone, much like a snake swallowing a frog, so it was critical to have medical support personnel standing by.

These days we have it made. They have all kinds of great sandwiches and salads and potatoes and fruit and everything else a growing boy (or girl) could want, but I still miss the good old days. In fact, all this reminiscing is making me hungry for something big and greasy from Burger Chef. Too bad it went the way of the dodo and the dinosaurs.

IS YOUR REFRIGERATOR RUNNING?

There was an archeological dig at our house over the weekend. No, they weren't excavating our backyard in search of ancient Indian arti-facts. Jan and I were just cleaning out the refrigerator.

I wouldn't say that we're exactly neatniks, but we try to keep a handle on our cold food inventory. However, stuff had accumulated to the point where you couldn't have crammed another quart of milk in there, so it was time to start purging. To say the least, I was a little shocked at the state of disarray (I like that word) of the old Kenmore.

The door was packed with dressings and condiments. You know how you sometimes open a bottle of ketchup in the pantry and then find the half-full one in the refrigerator? Well, you'd have figured that this big beast started its career on Noah's Ark. There were two open barbeque sauces, two ranch dressings, two mustards, two ketchups, two jalapeño peppers, blah, blah, blah. That didn't include five bottles of salad dressing that expired sometime before bin Laden took the bus.

Just out of curiosity, if you combine a half bottle of dressing that expired in 2017 with one that's good through 2019, you're fine until the end of 2018, right? Anyhow, we pitched and combined until the door was pretty well-organized, and then tackled the main body.

In our defense, old refrigerators weren't designed very well. They load from the front and unload from the front, so you can pretty much live off the nearest two or three strata (an archeological/geological reference) forever. As a result, there are things, terrible things that can grow and mutate and fossilize (more geo-archeology) in the back of any refrigerator without anyone noticing. To make matters worse, they now make plastic storage containers small enough to save a dab, and there were at least twenty smidges and fifteen dollops ripening in the deepest recesses.

There's never a medical examiner around to solve a meat puzzle when you need one. We could have used Ducky. There was one container that may have contained meatloaf. Either that or it was some leftover WWII K-rations. There was another that may have started life as beef tips and gravy. By the time I opened it, well, if you're a *Lord of the Rings* fan, and watched the main Orc (Ugluk) emerge from the brown slime . . . yummy.

Another discovery we made is that a bag of salad can actually purée itself with no need for slicing, dicing or use of a blender. All it needs is time. Also, do you know how a domestic pig, if released into the wild, can turn feral, growing coarse hair and tusks? Well, apparently a cabbage roll can undergo the same transformation if kept too long in captivity. Perhaps that's TMI.

I'll bet all this talk of food is making you hungry. If you're not busy this evening, slide on over for dinner. We're having leftovers.

THE STONE SOUP DU JOUR

Several years ago, I recall a great bit done by Andy Rooney, where he took a box of breakfast cereal, pulverized it into a fine powder, and built a tiny little Cheerios pyramid that costs about three bucks at the grocery store. I also remember one of the automakers putting "Corinthian leather" into their luxury vehicles. In retrospect, I think we were being snookered (I really like that word). The leather wasn't from anywhere near Corinth. In fact, one report I read said it might have even been part vinyl. That's right: pure Corinthian Naugahyde.

Anyhow, the world was simpler then, and I guess so was I. The stuff was being hawked by Ricardo Montalban, a very handsome and charming man with an accent, for heaven's sake, so I knew it had to be real. If I'd met Tom Sawyer in those days, I'm sure I'd have ended up whitewashing his fence.

Do you remember the story of stone soup? It had to be the first great scam. Three soldiers traveling in a foreign land have no food. They come to a village, set up camp in the square, and start cooking a kettle of water with nothing but stones thrown in. The villagers get curious, and the soldiers claim to be making stone soup. Imagine that! Ricardo could have sold Corinthian toilet paper to these maroons.

Anyhow, one villager thinks that it might be tastier with carrots, and tosses some in. Another suggests some salt and spices. Still another brings a cabbage. By the time the busybodies are done, they've added potatoes, beef, barley, onions and a bunch of other tasty goodies, and they all marvel at how delicious soup can taste when it's made only with stones! Yeah, I know. They were about 9.5 on the Dimwit Scale.

Well, a lot of water (or soup) has passed under the bridge since Ricardo was selling vinyl upholstery. I'd like to think I've seasoned a bit, and have reached the point where I'm a little too wise to get bamboozled (another good word) by sleight-of-hand or a fast-talking salesman. Apparently, I'm about a 9.6.

I was whipping up a batch of Hamburger Helper in a frying pan the other day, and that's when it hit me (an epiphany, not the frying pan). The box is very attractive, and it has a mouthwatering picture of the pasta dish you'll soon be devouring. So, you open it up, and for your $1.39 or whatever it costs, there's a packet of macaroni worth maybe a quarter, and a separate little pouch containing some seasonings and orange powder. That's it . . . that's all that's in there. It's all box and no dinner.

Oh, brother. I wasn't snockered, but I snickered because I thought I was too savvy to get snookered. This stuff is just modern-day stone soup. You pay a couple bucks for a cardboard picture and then add your own milk and hamburger. Would you like tomatoes? Sure, throw 'em in. Maybe some extra cheese? Be my guest. Black olives? Lovely! I think maybe I'll fire up a kettle in the front yard this evening and make a batch.

PLEASE PASS THE WORMS

Food was in the news this past couple of weeks. Well, more precisely, things that idiots are willing to put in their mouths for some attention made the headlines. Close to home, in the Holland area, some doofus (yes, that's the correct spelling) managed to reduce eight apartment units to their carbon derivatives by trying to burn the hair off a squirrel. Thankfully, the squirrel was already dead, and yes, he was planning to eat it, but this method of preparation is not preferred by firefighters or the hunting and gathering community. Normally, field dressing and cooking are considered to be separate tasks.

Next, a Florida man died after entering two very disgusting competitions on the same evening. The first was a superworm-eating contest. I don't actually know what a superworm is (and neither does my computer spell-check), but it may have come from the planet Krypton. Its name was probably Kal-eel, although only cast members from the *Big Bang Theory* would get the humor.

Anyhow, still hungry after a worm appetizer, our hero (Edward Archbold) then entered a giant cockroach-eating contest, which he won. Lucky guy. He later started vomiting and then died, which ruined his whole day. The report described it as "tragic and unexpected." To me, that's a bit like saying, "Man dies unexpectedly after drinking gasoline."

In our third installment, some college student looking for fame, glory, and cash agreed to lick a long section of a New York City subway handrail for a whopping eight bits. This is disturbing on so many levels. The article suggested that the people who don't wash up after using the restroom are the same ones who are later handling the railing. In short, he was sucking on an *E. coli* incubation center that was home to a few million other toxic organisms.

I guess this moron is still alive, but not due to common sense. It bothers me that this same young man might have a girlfriend, and he might even have plans to smooch her in the foreseeable future. College students do that. Meanwhile, the cash won't even pay for a bottle of Listerine.

Whatever happened to real food-eating contests? You know, stuff like Cool Hand Luke downing fifty eggs, or a blueberry pie eating contest, or those guys who scarf down 137 hotdogs? I was actually just in a chili cook-off. I didn't win but finished a respectable second, and my entry was noticeably lacking worms, cockroaches, and *E. coli* bacteria. With any luck at all, my wife might even give me a little kiss when I get home tonight.

CHAPTER 3

THE GREAT OUTDOORS

AS EASY AS RIDING A BIKE

We've all heard the expression that something is "as easy as falling off a log," or perhaps "as easy as pie." That must refer to eating the pie and not making the pie, because the whole crust thing has me befuddled (I like that word.)

Then there's the ever-popular "as easy as riding a bike." That was true when I was a kid. My bike was a big, clunky extension of my little, clunky self. It had a heavy-duty frame and wide tires and just one speed. It also had uncomplicated brakes that were activated by stomping on the pedals. We could speed down hills and cut through people's backyards and hop curbs and do wheelies and almost never got so much as a scrape. Ah, those were the good old days.

Since then, some demented, upscale, skinny little fitness buffs decided to create a by-gosh dream-cycle for people with too much time and lots of discretionary money on their hands. And so, I give you today's racing bike. It weighs less than a TV dinner, has a carbon-fiber frame, tires that are mere millimeters wide, disc brakes, twenty-seven speeds, cables sprouting from every orifice, high-tech toe clips, and a price tag rivaling that of a Lexus.

Let me see if I can explain the basic operation of this wonder of modern science. Pay attention, because the Space Shuttle is less complicated. Are you a multitasker? If not, you might skip the rest of this narrative and take up bowling. To begin with, examine your pedals. If they appear to have been replaced by something resembling the blade of a three-iron, then you have toe clips. You need to rush out and buy a pair of specialized bike shoes with hardware to match the clips. Get a helmet while you're at it. Go ahead, I'll wait.

Are you back? Marvelous. Now, start the bike forward, hop on, and clip both feet into place. You are now committed. You also better start pedaling. On each side of the handlebars, you'll see an intricate system of levers. On the right side is the back brake, and on the left side is the front. If you achieve twenty mph while going downhill and then slam on that front brake, you'll experience the joy of spontaneous cartwheels. This will entertain innocent bystanders.

Also on the handlebars, integrally connected to the brakes, are two more levers on each side for shifting the front and back sprockets up and down. If you wish to go from the large to the small chain ring in the front, you should simultaneously shift the matching lever controlling the back cluster. This will allow a smooth transition through the gears. Got it? Are you sure?

To summarize, you clip in, begin pedaling, build up speed, suddenly realize that you are approaching a busy intersection, downshift the rear gear cluster while simultaneously applying gentle pressure to the rear brake, come to a complete stop (now, here's where the real fun begins), and only then realize that your feet are still attached to the pedals. Rats. Then, while desperately trying to unclip, completely unaware that you are making panicky little noises normally associated with a seven-year-old girl, you'll do a perfect Arte Johnson and tip over on your non-dominant side. Once again, this will entertain any nearby spectators.

Then for the next fifteen minutes, lying on your side with your feet locked to the pedals, the frame pinning you to the ground, blood oozing from your left cheek, you will resemble a shackled Harry Houdini trying to extricate himself from some diabolical trap.

So, if you haven't broken your left wrist, and if your ego is still intact, you can get back on the literal and proverbial bike and give it another whirl. Perhaps I'll see you up on the White Pine Trail. If not, I'll look for your car in the bowling alley parking lot.

GOOD GAULEY, MISS MOLLY

Fall is Gauley season. You're probably thinking that you've never heard of a Gauley, and are wondering if it's some shirttail cousin of the white-tailed deer or an exotic upland game bird. Nope, it's neither. Actually, the Gauley is a river in West Virginia that's famous for its whitewater rafting. It's fed by discharge from the Summerville Dam, so fall flows are regulated to provide the optimum whitewater experience (that's marketing jargon for scaring the crap out of you).

Our group had done the New River (the Gauley's older sister) a couple times, so we figured we were ready for the big time. The upper Gauley is a pretty hairy and technical trip, with a number of Class 5 rapids (they only go up to 6) that can flip a raft in a split second. In short, it ain't no Disney ride.

We arrived at the headquarters early in the morning, and while munching on breakfast, went through a whole briefing session on wearing your brain bucket, bracing in, what to do if someone gets tossed into the drink, how to die with dignity, and so on. That's when the guides entered.

The rafting "community" in West Virginia reminds you of a collection of surfers or snowboarders. Most of them look like hippies, except they have shoulders like Gronk. A friend of mine in Mankato described the scene when the Minnesota Vikings came out of the locker room for pre-season training, and this was very much the same. They walked in, and a hush fell over the room as we looked in awe at this collection of lean, tanned river gods. The most impressive, someone who could have wrestled a crocodile into whimpering submission, was

Julia. She had that chiseled gaze and steely look that said her clients were as safe as a babe in her mother's arms.

The rest were cut from the same cloth, with long ponytails, beards, tattoos, and nicknames like Bear and Duke and Big John. Well, all but ONE of the rest. At the back of the pack, clean-shaven and pasty-white, looking more like Wally Cox than a mountain man, stood Randy. I thought he was somebody's kid brother, but he turned out to be a full-time high school teacher (I'm guessing Home Ec) and part-time rafting guide. He had puny little arms and lovely, delicate hands that were more suited to crocheting than schlepping six weekend warriors down a raging torrent. So, just guess who was assigned to our raft. Swell.

The trip turned into Bob and Bing (and Randy) on the *Road to Disaster*. We lost Dorothy Lamour in the first rapids. When you approach a section of heavy whitewater, the roar increases in a loud crescendo, and you watch each raft ahead of you disappear from sight as the gradient suddenly steepens. It's somewhat unnerving because it looks as though they've been swallowed up by the river.

Anyhow, the three big rules are to hang onto your paddle, so as not to rearrange the teeth of your neighbor, listen to your guide, no matter how wimpy he appears, and keep paddling, even in the serious stuff. Did I say rules? They're more like guidelines, really. We shot the first major rapids sideways because Randy the Rudder dropped his paddle. Then, going over Sweet's Falls, he managed to hang on to it, which wasn't all that helpful since he and the raft had already parted company.

The rest of the day was spent in similar fashion. We took all the nasty ones at forty degrees to port or thirty degrees to starboard, and sometimes even backward or upside down. Google "squeehawed," and you'll find a picture of our raft. At least all the customers in the other rafts were having a marvelous time. That's because they were with Duke or Big John, and also because of the entertainment we provided. I spent so much time in the water that my hands started looking like Randy's.

It's a gorgeous trip, with fabulous scenery, lots of wildlife, and a level of excitement unrivaled anywhere. If you go, ask for Julia.

OUT OF THE FRYING PAN

I just returned from one of those long 6-F (friends, family, fishing, fast food, fatigue) road trips that took me across half the country (if it's Friday, this must be Kansas). One new thing I encountered was a sign for an "Adult Superstore." I'm familiar with Super Walmart and Super Target. So, I'm guessing that you can get your groceries, tires, clothing, fine furniture, and porn all in one swell foop.

One of the highlights of this excursion was enjoying three days' fly-fishing in Colorado. The Frying Pan River runs into the Roaring Fork in the small town of Basalt, and the trout fishing (along with the scenery) is spectacular. The Fork is big and roily, with large, slippery boulders that make staying vertical in chest waders somewhat unlikely. As a result, there are long stretches of pristine, almost untouched water. The Frying Pan, on the other hand, is thirteen miles of gorgeous river paralleled by an access road, so it's pretty popular. It's also world-renowned, so you're bound to be sharing it with fifty or sixty of your closest friends.

Fortunately, I found a glassy section to call my own, and there was a nice hatch of Pale Morning Duns coming off, so I started flogging the water. Did I mention that these trout get a lot of attention? It wasn't their first rodeo. I'd drop a fly deftly (I like that word) into the perfect location, and you could almost hear an audible laugh. "Really? Is that the best you got? Hey, Al, it's another #16 Adams from Frying Pan Anglers. Man, what a loser." It's essentially the same response I used to get from girls in high school.

Anyhow, I stuck with it, and finally managed to fool a few of the nearsighted ones (trout, not girls), including a couple of rainbows and browns that had some serious shoulders on them. On the second day, my Uncle Phil and I went back to the Pan. To give you a visual, the river isn't real wide so I could cast to the far side wading twenty feet from the near shore. There was a high, steep bank (almost vertical) facing me, and behind me was a thick, brushy slope up to the road.

I was twenty yards above the point of a long, slender island that bisected the river, and Phil was fishing its lower end. As I fished, I heard a splash from behind the island and looked to the right just as a huge bear stepped out from behind the point, standing in the river less than thirty yards from me. She was ginormous. I found out later from a local guide that she tips the scale at over 400 pounds. Gulp. She froze, staring at me, bristled, and let go with a low growl. Uh-oh.

Have you ever had an "Oh, _____" moment? Insert your favorite fecal reference in the blank. Yes, I was having an "Oh, dung" moment. She was gorgeous, cinnamon brown in color, and the perfect shade to be a grizzly. As a stranger in a strange land, I didn't know if they had grizzlies around there (they don't) or if this was a light-colored black bear (it was). Feeling like second place on the food chain, I assumed the worst.

There was a big rush of adrenaline as I frantically tried to access my internal hard drive and decide on a course of action. Stop, drop, and roll? No, that's if you're on fire. Turtle down into the fetal position? Problematic, as I was in thigh deep water wearing chest waders. Turn and run, screaming like a little girl? I couldn't have outrun an overweight tortoise in those boots. Make yourself real big and try to fend her off with your buggy whip fly rod? Perfect.

As I contemplated my final moments on this earth, she made the decision for me. She simply turned right and walked effortlessly straight up that huge bank. Then, I found out why she didn't like my face (another high school flashback). Right in her footsteps were two adorable little cubs that had been behind her in the river.

In retrospect, I probably wasn't in any real danger. The growl was just her telling the kids to shut up and stop fooling around. She was being a good mom. Still, I'm pleased that (a) Neither myself nor my waders were reduced to the texture of pulled pork, and that (2) I didn't end up immortalized in a short blurb on page nine of the *Aspen Times*.

Anyhow, that's how I spent my summer vacation.

MUNGO'S REVENGE

When I was growing up, we had a next-door neighbor named Jerry Sietsma or Rietsma or some good Dutch name. Anyhow, we just called him Mungo. He was a nice enough guy, pretty quiet, and not brimming with pizazz (I like that word because it has three correct spellings). Anyhow, as far as I could tell, Mungo had only two functions in life. The first was going to his paying job (I pictured a cubicle in a rather sterile office somewhere), and the second was working in his yard. I mean, the guy was RELENTLESS. For six days a week, that was his entire life (this was Grandville – they rolled up the streets on Sunday).

Naturally, as all snotty little teenage boys do, my friend Dave and I teased him behind his back. If the wind caused the grass to ripple in the slightest, he (Mungo, not Dave) was out giving it (the lawn, not Dave) a haircut. Otherwise, he was weeding, feeding, edging, trimming, placing mulch, or hauling something in the wheelbarrow. Paraphrasing Mungo Jerry (hum along, if you like), "In the summertime, when the weather is high, you can mow the lawn 'till the moon is nigh." His place made the Grand Hotel grounds on Mackinac Island look like an abandoned lot.

My concern, and this is causing me some distress, is that I may have inadvertently become Mungo. I really didn't mean for this to happen. I was just trying to not have the worst lawn on the block and apparently overshot a bit. The recipe called for several trees to come out, a sprinkling system to be installed, a couple tablespoons of grass seed and a dollop of fertilizer, and suddenly we're living in the Emerald City.

The error of my ways was pointed out to me twice this week. First, my neighbor happened by, complimented me on how great the lawn looked, and then wryly said that he couldn't understand why people spend so much time watering and fertilizing and toiling just to create even more work. He's originally from India, where people are apparently born with a common sense gene.

Then, on Prairie Home Companion, Garrison Keillor commented that we do all this torturous work, not for ourselves, but to impress our neighbors. He suggested that it would be much simpler to just close the drapes. Indeed. Where were these Monday morning quarterbacks two years ago when I needed them?

In retrospect, the people I recall having the best yards also had four or five boys which they had cleverly scheduled to pop out on a two-year cycle. It was genius. By the time dad was good and sick of yard work and shoveling snow, the oldest one was ten, the baby was two, and mom and dad had live-in slave labor for the next sixteen years. After that, they could move to a condo in Florida. Talk about your Planned Parenthood.

I have a new appreciation for Mungo. I don't think the poor guy had any kids. Mine have long since moved away and left me with the lawn. That's gratitude for you. If they really loved me, they'd have been like those Cartwright boys on *Bonanza* and lived with us forever. Since that didn't happen, our only three choices are to adopt a ten-year-old boy, move to Florida, or treat the yard with some Vietnam-era surplus Agent Orange.

THE PERILS OF GARDENING

This is a public service message. I'm trying to get the word out, even go door-to-door if necessary, to warn people about the hazards of gardening. Yes, gardening. I know it seems like a rather wholesome and harmless activity. People till up rich soil, plant a plethora of parsley, peas, and potatoes, and in late summer reap the benefits of their labors. Sure.

Let's talk reality. First, you need to prepare the soil, so you buy a tiller. This is a sinister, gas-powered cross between a lawn mower and an octopus. Around our neck of the woods, there's an abundance of nice, stiff clay, so churning (turning, whatever) up the soil is about as easy as wrestling a bear. Next, you have to plant rows and rows of vegetables. This requires one to be crouched over in the shrimp position for hours at a time and may result in you permanently staring at your shoes.

So, you finally get all this stuff planted in May, and that's where the fun begins. You are now sequestered for the summer. Did I mention the weeding? It's relentless. You start in the southwest corner on Monday and finally finish the northeast corner on Saturday. Guess where you are on Monday. Go ahead, guess. Were you thinking about a summer vacation at the lake? I'm sorry, I thought you understood. There ARE no days off. It's like having a winter snowplowing business in Fairbanks.

Anyhow, you sweat and toil for hours and weeks and months, sacrificing your body and your time, and at long last your crop, the stuff dreams are made of, is ready to harvest. Yes, it is. And in one night, a herd of deer, rabbits, raccoons, and other assorted critters descends on your little plot of ground like a tsunami, ravenously devouring the fruits (and vegetables) of your labors. Groan.

Wait, cheer up. There is a handy math solution. Simply put, there is a finite number of available hours in any day. You can work your fingers to the bone growing your own greens, but then you'll have to buy your protein from the grocery store. Have you seen the price of steak lately? Or . . . (drum roll, please), you can take up fishing, harvest your own meat, and buy your vegetables instead. There isn't time for both, so choose the one that sounds like the most fun. Need a hint?

I hear what you're saying. Fishing is an expensive sport. Starting from scratch, you'll need rods and reels, a boat and motor, electronic fish finder, line, lures, flies, waders, vest, creel, and various other paraphernalia (I like that word). However, if you amortize (more math terms) this expense over, say, twenty years, those three brook trout you bring home for dinner every week drop to a paltry $29.99 a pound.

That's a small price for saving your back.

I hope this helps. Just say no to gardening. When the vegetables finally ripen, take a little trip to the Amish stand down the road. You can buy enough produce to feed your family for a week for about the same price as a fast food combo meal. Plus, it's on the way to the river.

ALL'S FAIR

I hate the fair. Well, actually, I love the fair. I suppose it's just one of those love/hate things, kind of like Sam Malone felt for his lovely (and often despised) Diane. Anyhow, it's that time of the year again, when hundreds of transient people in a big, traveling road show set up camp in our town and give us something new to do for a week.

When I say I love the fair, I mean I love the noise and commotion and smells (well, most of them) that fill the air during fair week. In the space of about a hundred feet, you can get elephant ears and caramel apples and bratwurst with onions, and even a complete barbecued chicken dinner. You can test your marksmanship by paying ten dollars for a chance to shoot a plastic duck and win a two-dollar stuffed animal. You can go watch local businesspeople try to coax a horse around the track (usually avoiding serious injury) in the celebrity harness race.

I also love people watching. There are hundreds of patrons browsing the grounds, and half of them you never see except during fair week. Where do they live? Where do they work? Some of them, dare I say, exude a rather frightening persona (I like that word), and people steer a wide berth around them as they walk through the midway. I remember one in particular, heavily tattooed with skull and crossbones and other intimidating body art, massive biceps the size of tree trunks, and both front teeth missing, causing a perpetual snarl, likely the result of some recent bar brawl. She was frightening.

On the hate side, there are the rides. Okay, call me a pansy, but people aren't meant to go round and round and up and down while simultaneously spinning like a top. Haven't you ever heard of centrifugal force? It's the physical phenomenon that causes your stomach to squash up against the starboard side of your ribcage and squeeze the aforementioned bratwurst back out into public view. It never looks as appetizing on its return flight.

There are two kinds of people in the world. The first love carnival rides. They could eat three chili dogs and a raw egg, do a double shift on a Tilt-a-Whirl and feel like a million bucks. I'm the poster boy for Type 2. After one minute on the Zipper, I spend the next two hours feeling like I have the flu. Why would one intentionally spend money to feel like crud? It's like volunteering for a repeat performance of your vasectomy.

The associated problem is that those who love rides aren't capable of just enjoying them with their own kind. Instead, they feel compelled to get the rest of us involved. It starts with friendly coaxing ("C'mon . . . you'll love it!"). When that doesn't work, they make remarks about your lack of intestinal fortitude. Finally, beaten, you agree to once again try the Octopus. When I was six, I hurled cotton candy after one of those rides, and I still can't eat it.

Anyhow, it's my mission (or curse) to provide years of residual entertainment for the rest of my family. "Did you see the look on his face? And he made that awful Uhhhhhhh sound!"

Maybe I'll see you there. It's my plan to shoot some plastic ducks, toss a few rings, pack myself full of the local cuisine and keep both feet firmly planted on the ground.

CHAPTER 4

LOVE AND MARRIAGE

WEDDED BLISTERS

A friend of mine (we'll call her Laura) is a nurse in Arizona who found the almost perfect guy and is ready to take the plunge. They decided that they could save money and better savor the whole experience by planning every facet of the wedding themselves. Hoo, boy.

In mathematical terms, organizing a wedding is like solving an equation with nine variables. In physics, it's like pushing a rope. In medical terms, it's like performing your own colonoscopy (it's a pain in the posterior).

You start by reserving the church and the minister for that perfect fall day, let's say October 1. You contact all the members of the wedding party and your immediate relatives and advise them to save the date. Everything is as smooth as butter. Uh, oh. This could be bad.

Next, you contact the caterer, and everything is still on target. This is worse, like when the kids are a little too quiet. That's when the church calls and tells you that the minister forgot to put his parents' surprise 50th-anniversary party on his calendar. You'll have to change it to the 8th. Nuts.

You check with the caterer, and the 8th still works for her. So, you re-contact the entire gaggle, and everyone can make it except the maid of honor, who leaves for Hawaii on the 7th. Rats. Back through the whole process, and after three iterations and sixty-eight phone calls, you settle on November 12. So much for the perfect fall day.

Now it's on to Phase 2, which is the guest list. Suddenly, aunts and uncles and cousins twice removed (you wish they'd stay removed) start popping up like whack-a-moles with copious suggestions about who should attend this GFO (Gala Festive Occasion). Just as suddenly, your guest list swells to 450, with names like, "Bob Smith +6." Who's Bob Smith? Why plus six? Does he have a harem? Is he bringing a litter of beagle puppies?

That day, you get an e-mail from the caterer inviting you to attend a taste test before you decide on a menu. Good idea. You make a reservation for a week from Friday.

The next day, you visit the florist and tell them you need bouquets for yourself and six bridesmaids. You also need boutonnieres for six groomsmen and something for the bride to throw at the single women. Probably not a baseball. They tell you it will be $3500. You assume that they'll be flying the flowers in on a chartered Lear from Tahiti.

The following day (eight days before your scheduled appointment), you receive another e-mail from the caterer thanking you for attending the taste test and complimenting you on your choice of entrees. Hmmmm. Somewhere, sometime, someone will be ordering last-minute pizza for 300 from Little Caesars. That's their problem.

Finally, it's time to adorn (I like that word) the wedding party. At this point, you really don't care anymore. Luckily, you have your mom's wedding dress. You're a shade under six feet. She's the height of a mailbox. You'll slouch. One problem solved.

Next, five out of six bridesmaids love the purple dresses. Only one really hates them. Purple it is. If she doesn't like it, tough. As for the tuxes, the groomsmen don't give a rat's rear end. They only want to know if there will be an open bar. You order charcoal gray. There, that was easy.

Not so fast, pard. Do you want light or dark charcoal? Vest or no vest? Textured or flat? Boxers or briefs? You notice that you seem to have developed a slight tic. It's probably nothing. Later that afternoon, you get a call from the church saying that asbestos has been discovered in the sanctuary, and the building is under strict quarantine until after the first of the year. They're very sorry.

I'm sad to report that the blessed event is on hold. Laura is currently under the care of a wonderful therapist. She should be released in a matter of months. . . possibly. When she gets out, she's changing her name to Penelope. The last word in Penelope is "elope."

MEN ARE FROM . . . CABELA'S

I hear there's a book out there, something about men being from Mars and women from Venus, which would partially explain why so many marriages are being flushed these days (and maybe why nobody seems to be able to speak English). Actually, men are from Cabela's and women are from Macy's, but it's the same principle. Anyhow, I'm not at all surprised about the failure rate, and there are a couple of plausible theories that could explain it.

One reason a marriage might have gone belly-up is the whole "opposites attract" theory. She was a good girl, great student, member of the glee club and marching band, class president, and stuff like that. He was a long-haired, hostile, anti-establishment rebel without a clue . . . and she was in LOVE. Do you remember those guys from high school? They had black leather jackets, cigarettes rolled up in their sleeves, boots, chains, and tattoos, and they rode around on their motorcycles like a pack of greasy-haired coyotes. Of course, they never actually DID anything. Mostly, they just liked to hang out and act tough. No education, no job, no ambition, and no prospects. So, she dropped out of college because he said it was for morons. They got married and moved into her uncle's trailer, and she worked two waitress jobs while he smoked dope and hung out with his smelly friends. Well, you know the rest. Three years and two kids later, she's wondering why he isn't Cary Grant.

The other reason these things never seem to work out is that the whole dating/courtship ritual is really a lot of false advertising. Enter your basic good ol' boy (Billy Bob), someone whose entire life is smoking, drinking, playing pool, staying out late, sleeping until noon, hunting, fishing, snowmobiling, bowling, and ALL in the same week while wearing the same dirty flannel shirt and underwear. One night he chances to meet a woman (Doris), and because it happens to be the same day he had his monthly shower and shave, she finds him (thanks to alcohol) to be less repulsive than normal, perhaps even tolerable. He, typically ignored and even shunned by the opposite sex, thinks she's the finest thing he's ever seen. So, for the next two months, he turns into Prince Charming. They go out on dates. He dresses up, sends her flowers, opens the car door, wears cologne, makes small talk over candlelit dinners, takes her to chick flicks, and couldn't be more attentive. They now have a spray that you can use on your 1992 Chevy to make it smell like a new car. It's the same principle.

So, they get married, and after a whirlwind honeymoon, they adjourn to his previous life. Three months later, she wakes up next to an unemployed grizzly bear with a three-day beard and the fragrant aroma of sour mash whiskey oozing from his pores, and she can't figure out what happened to her little Snookums.

I've watched Disney flicks and those National Geographic specials. There are some great cameramen out there who film hours of video following giant anacondas or a pride of lions or even a family of golden eagles. What we need is a new service, a private agency that can provide candid Spycam videos of Billy Bob in the wild, so Doris can see how he REALLY lives. We want her to witness his general disdain for personal hygiene products, his heavy use of chewing tobacco, his foul language, and his hot temper when he comes home from drinking with the boys (which is only every night). That way, unsuspecting Doris can kick the tires, so to speak, and make an informed decision about spending the rest of her life with this bum. Meanwhile, if you're a single guy, and you notice an inordinate number of people around you who seem to be sporting video equipment . . . don't be alarmed.

I, DENISE, TAKE YOU, GINGER

I recently received a very interesting letter from a woman (we'll call her Denise) who finds herself on the horns of a dilemma. With all the turmoil concerning civil unions and strange bedfellows, she feels this is a perfect time to throw one extra curveball into the mix. Essentially, she wants to marry her dog.

Now, before you fly off the handle, please hear me out. First, the woman's husband passed away some time ago, so there is no issue of bigamy. Denise and her dog (Ginger) have been together for eight years, and are completely devoted to each other. The dog has always slept in the same bed with Denise (and with her husband, before his passing). If you talk to their friends, all you'll hear are wonderful testimonials of individual bravery, gentle disposition, and a wonderful temperament around children. I understand that the dog is equally impressive.

Unfortunately, there is one issue that may bother some of you. The dog is female, and there is plenty of discussion these days about same-sex marriages. However, Denise assures me (and she has always been a truthful person) that the relationship is purely platonic, and that they are only best friends. Yes, I know they share the same bed, but it's only because the dog is a perfect electric blanket (Denise has cold feet). The main reason for formalizing their relationship is so that Ginger can be included on her health insurance and other benefits. Those vet bills can be pretty steep, especially in the case of an older dog, and Denise is on a fixed income.

The only other issue is that of children. Both parties have expressed an interest in extending their love to someone they can raise and nur-ture. Therefore, if they are allowed to marry, I wouldn't be surprised if they decided to adopt. Initially, this concerned me, until I found out that they hope to take in a litter of puppies in need of a good home. Even without a man around the house, I'm confident that the pups will do just fine, and they'll be raising their legs on the furniture in no time.

Therefore, as odd as it sounds, I find that I'm a hundred percent in favor of Denise's intended nuptials. If the partner in question were a cat, especially a male, I wouldn't be in favor of matrimony. I'd be afraid that he'd be aloof and reclusive, prowling around until all hours when she really needs someone at home. Such a marriage couldn't help but fail. Of course, if we allow Denise to marry her dog, it may open a whole new can of worms or create a fine kettle of fish or some other related animal cliché. Still, some animals might actually make pretty good partners. If you married a goat, you'd never have to pay for garbage pickup, but they are somewhat lacking in social graces. My dear friend M.L. owns a pack (herd, gaggle, whatever) of llamas, but let's make that a story for another day

MARRIAGE ADVICE FOR THE FRAZZLED POLYGAMIST

A good friend of mine, after suffering through the agony of his second divorce, proclaimed, "Bob, the next time I'm thinking of getting married again, I'm going to find a woman I really can't stand and buy her a house." Okay, maybe that's a bit cynical, but it points out that it takes a lot of time and energy and commitment to keep just one marriage intact and partner happy.

That brings us to today's topic. Every couple of years, some idiot gets arrested for polygamy, and it turns out that he has five different wives (each unaware of the others) stashed away in Atlanta, Detroit, Topeka, Phoenix, and San Diego. I'm sorry, but I just don't get it. Talk about too much of a good thing. Aside from living a complete lie and having to make five different house payments, he would have to spend every waking minute on the road, and totally give up important manly pursuits like fishing, golfing, and watching hockey. He would also have five perpetually unhappy spouses, all complaining that he needs to spend more time at home.

In a related story, a Saudi man, Judaie Ibn Salem (we'll just call him "Jud"), lost not only his pride but a sizable chunk of his nose when he was assaulted by both of his wives. As in two. Apparently, there was an argument over dividing up his house, so he first accused the two women of being rude and impolite, and then jokingly threatened to marry a third woman if they didn't straighten up. This did not have the desired effect. Instead of being intimidated into submission, these modern Arab women joined forces, went ballistic and carved him up like a Halloween pumpkin.

As a result, our pal Jud told the *Shams* newspaper (that's Saudi for "Pioneer") that the only way to restore his dignity would be to actually follow through with his threat and take a third wife. Huh? He then lamented, "I don't know what I'm going to lose next if I do that." I have some thoughts regarding other protrusions, but we'll go with, "what's left of your mind."

This guy needs serious counseling. If I had a pair of pet bobcats, and they had just mauled me, I wouldn't solve the problem by purchasing a third. Okay, bad analogy. I'm not saying women are like bobcats. Let's change directions. Another dear friend of mine, whose family members have a habit of bringing home dogs, cats, birds, hamsters, rabbits, and other assorted animals, has a new pet policy in his house. Basically, it reads, "One in, two out." Perhaps I should put him in touch with Jud. Therefore, in honor of the Judmeister and anyone else out there contemplating slow suicide by multiple marriages, I'd like to offer some free advice:

- Marriages are very much like certain distilled spirits. If you have more than one at a time, your brain turns to mush.
- Never insult wives carrying sharp weapons.

- If you can't keep one woman happy, your odds won't improve with three.
- With several women in the house all watching Lifetime, your ESPN days are numbered. Actually, they're over.
- The honey-do list just grew exponentially. You may as well sell your clubs, your boat, and all the rest of your toys.
- Don't.

I hope this helps. If not, best of luck in Saudi Arabia or Utah or wherever . . . but you'll be back.

IF YOU LOVE ME, JUST DON'T ASK

We've all heard it, either in our own lives or from people around us. Typically, one spouse decides to test the other's true level of commitment (or wants to find out who actually wears the pants) by suggesting, "If you really love me, you'll _____." Invariably, the task or chore listed in the blank results in great inconvenience or embarrassment or having to sacrifice something really important. It's a bit like when your dad uses your full name ("Robert Eastley, come over here."). If someone begins a sentence with, "If you really love me," what follows can't be good.

In my opinion, the secret to a happy marriage is to never ask your other half to do things which are contrary to his/her nature. I'm a happily married guy because that certain someone in my life never insists that I perform the kinds of tasks listed below:

At the top of the list is asking your husband, as long as he's going to the store, to pick up certain feminine hygiene products. There is no excuse to run out of these things. The reason for purchasing them is not an unforeseen event, like a tsunami or the attack on Pearl Harbor. Every woman is aware that she'll be in need of certain items at specific time coordinates in the foreseeable future and should plan accordingly.

There is no reason for any male to be involved at any level.

Next is shopping. Most women, especially those who have been married for any length of time, realize that our attention spans are about as long as a high-sticking penalty, and actually use shopping as a means to get AWAY from us and commune with their peers. Bless their hearts. However, I've noticed that some of the younger, less-seasoned brides feel that the secret to a successful marriage is to do absolutely EVERYTHING together. Believe me when I say that, even if he smiles and dutifully tags along, he's not enjoying it. We like to buy, not shop. Please don't make us go.

Karaoke: There are two kinds of people in the world. Some just love the sounds emitting from an intoxicated person singing almost on-key, and the rest of us would rather get poison ivy or plunge a toilet. If you truly love someone, torture isn't humane, so don't force them to accompany you to a karaoke bar.

Fashion advice: My only fashion decision is deciding which gray T-shirt to wear with my blue jeans. If you ask me which ensemble looks best on you, I just know I'm not going to give you the answer you're hoping for, and you'll probably end up wearing the other one, anyway.

Reunions of all types: Whether it's for the Class of '70 or the family type, there's always one spouse who is directly involved and the other who's an extra appendage and doesn't know anybody. This is tricky business. The first person wants to make an evening of it and catch up on old times. If she insists that her husband stop whining and entertain himself, she's pushy. If he starts looking at his watch about forty-five minutes after arriving, he's a self-centered jerk. There's only one real solution. Drive separate cars.

In an old movie, a young lady told her preppy boyfriend that, "Love means never having to say you're sorry." Horse dung. True love is allowing your spouse to skip the family reunion, and only demanding a short guilt trip in return.

CHAPTER 5

ANIMAL PLANET

BIG DOGS

Our universe is driven by a number of natural laws, including those of physics (you can't push a rope), thermodynamics (waders only leak in March and November), and chemistry (hot women don't date geeks with pocket protectors). However, there also exists a Law of Proportionality. I'm not sure it's been written down anywhere, but everybody knows about it. In a nutshell, this law states that those with all the money get to own the biggest toys, like SUV's that guzzle more fossil fuels than an aircraft carrier. They live in mall-sized mansions, send their spoiled kids to the most prestigious universities, hang out at country clubs where the greens fees could buy a Rolex, dine on caviar and other delicacies that nobody can pronounce, and basically just live larger than the general population.

However, it has come to our attention that a certain segment of the population either didn't get the memo or merely chooses to ignore it. One of my running friends (we'll call her Beth), was recently out on a long training run and became painfully aware of some sort of weird inversion in the whole scheme of things. As she put it, she was somewhere out in rural America, about two miles past the middle of nowhere, when she was accosted by a dog. Well, it may have been a dog. Based on her testimony, it was like some monstrous cross between a timber wolf, a rhinoceros, and a tyrannosaurus rex. She wasn't sure if she was going to be mauled, rammed, or devoured.

The entire scene put a bit of a damper on the serenity and ambiance of her run, as she spent the next ten minutes dancing around and trying to fend off this mutant from Jurassic Park. Meanwhile, the owner (not wishing to miss a minute of Judge Judy) attempted to be as useless as possible, periodically calling out through the open window, "Here, Manson, come here, boy," and "Don't worry, he won't hurt you."

Finally, just when Beth thought the end was near, he (Manson, not the owner) became distracted by a passing vehicle and took off in pursuit of fresh meat. This gave Beth the opportunity to start breathing again and survey her surroundings. She said the guy was living in the decaying remains of an old mobile home about the size of your average ice shanty. It looked like something you might bulldoze after a hurricane. However, parked in front were three brand new snowmobiles, worth almost as much as she makes in a year, a four-wheeler (presumably for dragging home the mangled remains of whatever Manson could run down), and a super-duper extended-cab pickup truck. This thing was large enough to haul a good-sized Apostolic Lutheran family, with fancy mirrors, and trailer hitches and winches and all sorts of expensive gizmos.

In her words (I'm paraphrasing), how can a person living in a tiny little shack with no visible means of support afford to own a dog the size of a Sherman tank, a truck bigger than the dog, and the most expensive toys of anyone in the county? It's rather intriguing and makes one wonder if he really is who he appears to be. Perhaps the gentleman is an entrepreneur, and has a cash crop, as it were, growing in an undisclosed location on his back forty. Or, perhaps he's an eccentric millionaire recluse, some sort of backwoods Howard Hughes. He might even be an ex-Enron executive trying to maintain a low profile. Regardless, as long as Manson keeps supplying him with generous quantities of fresh venison, wild turkey, groundhog, coyote, and the occasional leg of mailman, I'm thinking that the guy could go a long time without ever having to surface.

ANIMAL MAGNETISM

Picture this. You just finished a glass of Merlot while watching the late news, and now it's time for bed. You slide under the covers, nice and cozy, and start to drift off. Suddenly, THREE GUYS appear in your bedroom, haul you out of bed, drag you, kicking and screaming, into the street, tape your mouth shut, smack you in the face a couple times, stretch you out to measure your height with a tape measure, and then deposit you in a nearby shrub. Then, as they're walking away, you hear one of them say, "Boy, he was really cranky." You lie there a while, and then finally extract yourself and stagger back into the house, wondering what the heck just happened.

Not plausible, you say? Actually, this essentially describes the plot of almost every one of these new-generation, "close encounter with a large carnivore" shows. I just watched one, where a giant anaconda had been seen frequenting this large, swampy pond, and the show's star (a new-age Marlin Perkins) was sure it was sleeping in the mud at the bottom of the pond. So, what would you do? I'd get in the truck and head for dry ground . . . maybe Kansas, but not our hero. He, along with his weekly guest, some poor slob who really hated snakes, decided it was important to remove this bad boy (which had just finished its glass of Merlot) from its nice, cozy bed. But . . . first, they had to FIND him.

"How," you might ask, "would they do that?" It's quite simple, really. The two of them removed their shoes and waded around in this leech-and-mosquito-infested glop, attempting to locate the snake with their toes! Gosh, what a good idea! Anyhow, the host was loving every minute of this insanity, while the new guy (Jim, Tonto, whatever) looked as though he needed some serious blood-pressure medication. Well, they finally found it (the snake, not the medication), and Jim proceeded to make whiny, whimpering noises while Marlin tried to locate the end that didn't have teeth.

When I tell you that this animal was impressive, we're talking Sumo Snake. It was as big around as Raymond Burr, and you could have used it to measure first downs on Monday Night Football. So, they managed to find the non-business end, and the two of them, with the help of half the film crew, proceeded to drag the poor thing tail-first from the bog, while it tried desperately to crawl back into bed. Finally, after a ten-minute tug of war, they held up the giant beast for all to admire just like a trophy sailfish, and then simply let it go. As it swam away, I'm almost sure I heard it muttering, "Sheeesh, what was that all about?"

The only trouble with these reality shows is that they don't have any real purpose. I can understand tranquilizing grizzly bears to relocate them to less populated areas, or attaching a radio collar to an Upper Peninsula moose in the interest of monitoring and protecting the animal. Instead, we're stuck with the kind of fool who bops a croc on the nose, and then dances back while the thing lunges at his throat, just to show us that he can bob and weave like Barry Sanders. Oh, well, as our illustrious hosts gradually age and slow down, and the venomous animals they're provoking don't, I suspect these shows will eventually die of natural causes.

THE WORLD'S OLDEST FATHER

This just in from New Zealand: They claim to be home to the world's oldest father. Perhaps it's their temperate climate, or maybe it's something in the water. Or, more likely, it's because this particular dad isn't exactly human. He's Henry, the 111-year-old tuatara, a homely little reptile with a spiny back whose closest cousins are lizards and snakes. Regardless, he and his bride, Mildred, produced a dozen eggs last month, and are just waiting around for their offspring to hatch.

While this is difficult to confirm, it appears that the previous record for being the world's oldest parents belongs to Mr. and Mrs. Mondello, Larry's parents on the old *Leave it to Beaver* series. Larry was Beaver's whiny little friend whose face was always covered with ice cream or chocolate.

We never saw Mr. Mondello, as he was always in Cincinnati or some other exotic location on business. However, at the time that Larry appeared to be seven or eight, his mother looked like a seventy-something version of Aunt Bea. As a little kid watching the show, this made perfect sense to me. However, now that I have a better grasp of physiology and math, I'm wondering if perhaps we should contact Ripley.

Anyhow, getting back to Henry and Mildred, I have to question the wisdom of starting a family at this late stage in life. In fact, this may be the oldest documented midlife crisis. How is someone who was born when Grover Cleveland was in office going to find the energy to chase after twelve kids? Heck, he'll be a doddering old geezer of almost 130 when they graduate from high school!

Interestingly, a unique characteristic of tuataras is that they have a parietal, or third eye. Well, the old boy is going to need eyes in the back of his head when they all turn thirteen at the same time and start sneaking out of the house and slithering around with their teenage buddies.

Let's consider all the other complications related to having a litter of twelve-tuplets. Transportation will be a huge issue. Henry and Mildred will probably have to buy a cargo van or a school bus just to haul them around. Picture all those kids needing to be taxied to soccer and football and band and choir practices at different times. Plus, they'll ALL undoubtedly need braces and orthodontic work. And what happens when they turn sixteen and all start driving at the same time?

Then, one has to consider the daily mountain of laundry and trying to feed such a large gaggle. If they're boys, they'll eat their parents out of house and nest. But what if they have twelve girls? That could be even worse. Where are mom and dad going to find the cash to pay for a dozen weddings?

Let this be a friendly warning to all you young bucks out there who are in your late 90s and thinking about ditching your wives and starting a new family with some sweet young thing. Instead of spending your golden years playing golf and pursuing the wily trout, you're likely to find yourself in the full-time role of head cook and taxi driver. You may wish to reconsider.

JUST A LITTLE MONKEY BUSINESS

Wanted: SWF. Actually, in this case, it's an SFG, short for Single Female Gorilla. Strange as it may sound, India only has one gorilla. Uno, no dos. Rumor has it that Polo is tall, handsome, bilingual, available, and REALLY frustrated. That's because the nearest potential mate isn't even in the same time zone. In the words of Telly Savalas, "There's no booze, there's no broads, there's no action!" They should probably change his name from Polo to Solo.

The problem seems to be geography. India doesn't want to send him abroad, because he's their only big, hairy primate. Other zoos don't have any extra females, so the poor guy is SOL (Silverback Outta Luck). Since gorillas are social animals that typically live in family groups, he's unhappy and depressed. His only joys in life are bathing and trying to find food, which his keeper hides in bamboo or in blocks of ice. What kind of a sadistic jerk would hide a banana in a block of ice?

Well, folks, it's been eight years since he (Polo, not the keeper) last had a romantic fling, and a guy can only take so many baths (or in his case, cold showers). Regardless, solitary confinement is a pretty harsh sentence for a mild-mannered monkey (fine, he's an ape) who never did anyone any harm. These people need to scare up a girlfriend for him before he goes crackers.

I know what you're thinking, but I'm not suggesting that they hire a hooker or anything. I'm just thinking that he could put in for a sabbatical, go on vacation, take a Tour de Zoos. If you check your world map, you'll note that India is more or less adjacent to Nepal, Sri Lanka, and China. As it turns out, the zoo in Beijing is reputed to have a magnificent gorilla exhibit.

So, for all you fans of *Animal House*, I'm thinking road trip. First, they need to rent one of those snazzy motor homes, a huge one like the Taj Mahal on wheels. Then, they'll need a team of beauticians to get Polo all spruced up. Picture him after a hot shower, a manicure, and a pedicure. He'll probably need a little Grecian Formula to bring back his old hair color and leave just a hint of silverback. Next, if they trim his mustache and buy him one of those satin smoking robes, he'll be as dashing and debonair as a big, knuckle-dragging David Niven. Finally, splash a little after-shave on his face, and he'll be as irresistible as a puppy.

Once he's on his quest, he'll be just like Bob and Bing on the road to Beijing, on the prowl for Dorothy Lamour in a fur coat. However, the transition from lonely hermit to man about town may be a rather dramatic one. Picture him stepping out of his fancy ride at the front gate of some zoo in China, an international playboy escorted by his entourage. The women will swoon. He'll be an instant sensation.

Of course, there may be a downside to all of this. Once the female gorillas in these other cities get a look at Polo the Magnificent, the local talent in their own zoos will be about as thrilling as a plate of left-overs. Someone from out of town always seems so much more exciting and attractive. Would you want a date with Goober Pyle if Robert Redford just made the scene?

I don't have a solution for the male gorillas in those other zoos. The poor saps are likely to be ignored and suffer the same lonely fate as Polo. It looks like they'll need a fleet of motor homes so they can take the whole gaggle on the road. Next stop, Morocco.

WHY DID THE CHICKEN?

Some friends of ours (we'll call them Liz and Jeremy) are chicken farmers. Actually, they both have real jobs, but they live in a cool place in the woods with lots of extra space and decided on a new hobby.

Their little venture has been an education for me. They asked me if I knew how many kinds of chickens there were, so I rattled off fried, broiled, baked, Kiev, fricassee, and the like. Actually, silly me, they were referring to the various breeds, like Leghorn, Plymouth Rock, Rhode Island White, and Sumatra. There are about a gazillion different ones, and they're even rated by temperament and color of eggs, which can be white, brown, blue, and speckled. Get a big flock, and you won't have to color any Easter eggs this year!

The other rather interesting factoid is that there are two basic types. Baby chicks are either meat chickens or layers. I asked how you could tell the difference, and Liz told me they either have a little "L" or "M" tattooed on their chests. It turns out that the laying hens are smaller and produce a lot more eggs, and the meat chickens grow more quickly and have much larger breasts. That's why their layers have cute names like Hendrix and Chicken Little, and the bombshell meat mommas are named Stormy, Raquel, and Dolly.

It occurred to me that life could either be pretty cushy or rather traumatic for a chicken. First, if you find yourself in a box being shipped to Liz and Jeremy's, you have a life expectancy that's easier to measure in hours than in days. They have a herd of assorted critters living in their woods, like foxes, raccoons, and bobcats, that view a new baby chick shipment as drumstick takeout. The raccoons are especially adept at breaking into almost any enclosure, so being sent to this address is like jumping off the first troop transport at Omaha Beach.

If you survive the first couple of days, you then have to start dealing with the insignia on your chest. The laying chickens have it made in the shade. For them, the "L" stands for "Lucky." They have a big, fancy resort condo with air conditioning, color TV, gourmet feed, and lots of space to wander around and gab with their friends. All they have to do is produce a daily egg or two, and they're treated like British royalty.

The meat chickens are more like death row inmates. They're kept in a Quonset hut segregated from the prissy little layers, just because they behave like bullies and eat all the food. Well, I don't blame them. Life is hardly a bowl of cherries on the Green Mile. Every day they wake up wondering whose number will come up next, whose habeas will be the next corpus, just like lobsters in a tank at one of those fancy seafood restaurants.

If I were a meat chicken, I'd be looking for some steel wool to get that dang thing off my chest. Then, I'd find an egg to sit on and hope I could take credit for it.

Meanwhile, ladies, have you recently spent too much time watching the Kardashians or *Jersey Shore*? Are you considering a facelift or maybe saving up for breast enhancement surgery? If so, you may want to heed the story of Liz and Jeremy's voluptuous (I like that word) meat chickens. You could wake up in a Quonset hut with your number being called.

HAVE YOU HUGGED YOUR SQUIRREL TODAY?

It's January. It's dreary, and it's cold, and the residual fallout from Christmas hangs over all of us like a big, gray cloud. Wow, thanks, Debbie Downer. Anyhow, the Christmas season is such an upbeat time, with food and friends and family and frolic, and then, just like that, it's over. Suddenly, there's nothing to do but shovel the driveway in the dark before you go to work in the dark and come back home in the dark.

The problem is that there's nothing exciting to look forward to. That greatest of all holidays, Woodchuck Day, is on the distant horizon, and January drags on like a three-hour budget meeting. Well, not anymore. I just discovered a major cause for celebration. As it turns out, January 21 is ... drum roll, please ... bigger drum roll ... National Squirrel Appreciation Day. I told you this was big. Not only that, but it's also Granola Bar Day and Hugging Day. And if that's not enough excitement, the 24th is Beer Can Appreciation Day, Compliment Day, and Peanut Butter Day. Be still, my heart.

It's time to pull ourselves out of our funk and carpe diem. We need to create one massive GFO to blend all of these into the holiday of holidays, an excuse for sending another Hallmark greeting card, as it were. I, for one, appreciate beer cans. They're worth ten cents apiece, and without them, there'd be beer all over the floor. What's not to like?

We have a plethora of black squirrels around our house. They're wild, but over time, they've lost a lot of their shyness and developed a tolerance for humans. Often times they'll come right up on the porch in search of a snack. I'm embarrassed to admit it, but I don't think I've truly appreciated the little guys like I should. I certainly haven't paid them enough compliments. Well, that's about to change.

As for granola bars, I used to do a lot of running, and after every event, they were offered as a post-race treat. There was a variety of flavors, including Oats and Honey, Kale and Okra, Sawdust and Elmer's Glue, and other delicious blends. Sorry, but I can't do it. I've appreciated enough for ten people. But, I'm all over peanut butter, the crunchier the better, and nothing beats a good hug.

So, let's create a new holiday. Pennsylvania makes a big deal of celebrating their oversized muskrat. Why shouldn't Michigan get in on the fun? *Carpe* from the Latin means to seize, and *sciurus* is the word for squirrel. So, we'll call it "National *Carpe Sciurus* Day," loosely translated as "Hug Your Squirrel Day."

To properly observe this holiday, including all that beer can, granola bar, peanut butter, and other stuff, start by rescuing a can of your favorite malt beverage from the refrigerator. Next, pay a compliment to your wife as you pass by on your way to the hammock on the back deck. Before getting comfortable, spread a copious (I like that word) quantity of peanut butter on a granola bar, and set it on the porch railing. Now, just relax and sip on that cold beer until an unsuspecting *sciurus* hops up on the deck to investigate. Finally, once he sticks his curious little nose into that peanut butter, leap into action, *carpe* the little critter by the back of the neck, and give him a great big hug. You can be sure he'll feel appreciated.

I'm not sure if there's such a thing as preventative rabies shots, but it might be worth investigating before you begin this new holiday observance. Anyhow, enjoy the day. Carpe on, Garth.

THE BEST-DRESSED ROAD KILL

I don't remember if it was James Dean or Jimmy Dean or Jan and Dean, but some bad boy teenage heartthrob once said, "Live fast, die young, and leave a handsome corpse." As it turns out, these were prophetic words, especially for raccoons and possums and other suicidal road-crossers near the city of Edwardsville in southern Illinois.

Apparently, a graduate art student (and amateur mortician) named Jessica May has been prowling the roads around this city in search of the roadkill *du jour* and then has been dressing them up in human baby clothes, painting their claws with nail polish, and even adorning them with gold paint. Then, she just leaves them by the side of the road to be noticed and admired by the passing public.

In an interview, the young lady claimed that she wanted to see if people would slow down and pay more attention to these animals if they were given human attributes. Actually, I think she just has a toenail fetish, but the living critters won't hold still long enough for a pedicure.

Miss May's (the grad student, not the centerfold) heart appears to

71

be in the right place, but her logic seems a little out of whack. First, none of us intentionally hits a thirty-pound raccoon with hams the size of a small hog's. It's just that every time we bob, they weave, and ultimately, they end up sharing the same time and spatial coordinates with our left front tire. It's sad but unavoidable.

Now, if you take that same raccoon, the one with a tire-mark tattoo on his head, paint his toenails red, and put him in a little pink outfit once worn by your niece, all you'll accomplish is horrifying the passersby, who will now be gawking at this poor dead creature instead of looking at the road ahead. Meanwhile, an unsuspecting skunk wanders out, and . . .

I believe the problem goes way beyond scaring the daylights out of passing motorists. Remember when your mom told you to always wear clean underwear in case you had to go to the hospital? Well, picture a mother raccoon saying, "Rocky, be sure to comb your fur and put on a nice outfit. You never know when you might get plastered by a passing bus."

The point is, once the current crop of teenage rodents (and marsupials) sees their buddies all spruced up by the side of the road, they're going to demand equal treatment. They'll be taking out credit cards so they can purchase expensive outfits, and soon they'll be up to their pointy little ears in debt. Plus, they'll be spending all day in the bathroom putting on hair gels and press-on claws and colognes, and going WAY too heavy on the makeup and eyeshadow, just so they can look like a four-legged version of some television heartthrob.

After that, it's a short transition to body piercings, tattoos, dreadlocks, and wearing their little trousers down to their knees. Mark my words, within five years, we'll have an entire generation of nocturnal creatures that looks like Bob Marley, and we'll owe it all to Jessica May.

So, the next time you're out for a Sunday drive, instead of counting cows, keep an eye out for rodents by the side of the road. And, if you should happen to see a groundhog wearing sunglasses and a Hawaiian shirt, looking like the title character from *Weekend at Bernie's*, don't be alarmed. It just means that somewhere on the road ahead, there's a young lady with Illinois plates and a trunk full of kids' clothing looking for her next masterpiece.

CHAPTER 6

QUIRKY PEOPLE

MISTER ED

Hey, Wilbur. There's been an awful lot of media attention lately devoted to ED. My first thought, considering the current political climate, was that perhaps it stood for Election Drivel. However, further analysis makes me think perhaps it's some guy named Ed. Ed Norton? Ed Asner? Mr. Ed? I'm at a loss.

Most of the television coverage seems to focus on women, beautiful women, wandering around the house in their nightgowns with a distant, rather longing look in their eyes. My first thought was that they were pining for ED, but it seems that they are somehow trying to get rid of him. This confused me even more. Why don't they like him? Perhaps he's a former boyfriend who won't take the hint or a distant uncle who came to visit and overstayed his welcome.

Again, according to these commercials, it seems that the most effective way to get ED out of your life is with a big, blue pill. I suppose it's some sort of strong tranquilizer. You slip one in his coffee and drop him off at Aunt Margaret's house after he passes out.

The other way to solve this odd equation has something to do with bathing. Apparently, an effective way to eradicate Uncle ED is to hide in the backyard and not answer the door. For some reason, you need a pair of matching bathtubs sitting side by side, and you and your wife can sit in them, holding hands, and hoping ED gets tired of ringing the front doorbell. If he leaves, problem solved. If he persists, you simply hunker down and pretend you're in a foxhole.

My wife and I thought we should try it, but finding a pair of matched clawfoot tubs on eBay is difficult. Besides, it takes about twenty trips hauling water from the bathroom to the backyard, which is way more grueling than we imagined. By then the water is cold, and there are mosquitoes, and then there's the BIG issue of getting from the house to the tub unnoticed. So, we finally just gave up and went back inside. I'm sure the neighbors were pleased.

The other part of this convoluted issue deals with the time element. Perhaps I wasn't paying close enough attention (as usual), but it seems that, if Uncle ED stays more than four hours, you're supposed to contact your physician. My doctor is a heck of a nice guy, but his physique is more like that of a distance runner than a bouncer. I'm not sure he'd be up to evicting a large, problem relative, and I rather doubt if he'd be willing to try. Wouldn't it make more sense to call the police?

Anyhow, you can see my dilemma. If any of you can shed some light on this peculiar topic, please feel free. Why is the problem relative always named ED? Why are these lonely women lounging around in their underwear? Could the blue pills be used to eradicate other problem intruders, like pamphlet-bearing door-to-door religious cult members? Why does anyone need two bathtubs? Why am I so flummoxed (I like that word)?

THE BOSS

No, this isn't a Bruce Springsteen article. It's about that special person you hang out with forty or fifty hours a week. This is the guy who looks sarcastically at his watch when you walk in two minutes late from lunch, and the reason you start dreaming of Friday at five on Monday at nine. It's your pal . . . the boss. Actually, I've always felt that there are two kinds of bosses in the world. The first, like some of our better presidents, has to be dragged into a leadership role. He'd be much more comfortable working effectively in his current capacity, but he's needed, so he agrees to serve. The other type is a climber, typically shallow, has no interpersonal skills, and is despised by his subordinates. This type longs to be placed in a position of power, views himself as a natural-born leader, is ALWAYS right, and has delusions of adequacy.

Like most of you, I've enjoyed some bosses that I'd be proud to treat to lunch on Boss's Day, some I'd rather just ignore, and only one that I'd have enjoyed watching hang by his feet while someone administered the piñata treatment. That particular individual was named Earl. It was the summer of 1972, and we were working in a factory where the "Early Bird" was the designated Frank Burns. Everybody despised Earl. Those who didn't hate Earl hadn't met Earl.

First, let me set the stage a bit. Earl was the Prince of the Paint Room in a large office furniture plant. The paint room was where they sent you if you were too old, too ugly, too disturbed, or too crude to infest other areas of the plant. Our merry band included a pervert, a sweet old guy who wandered around and did nothing, a freak (he used to come in on Monday mornings and tell us about the orgies he and his wife hosted), a crazy little guy with a VERY loud voice who only knew words starting with "F," and a green college kid there for the summer (me). It was peachy. The paint room was hot, poorly ventilated, and the place where we mixed and pumped paint to all parts of the plant. The place was fume city. We slathered the floors, the walls, and ourselves with acetone, toluene, and more carcinogens than I can remember. Actually, I'm kinda surprised that I'm still here.

That summer, we worked from six thirty a.m. to five thirty p.m. every day. Mornings were dreadful. I had to leave home at five thirty to be in the locker room by six and change into the company grays. Enter Earl. This guy swooped in every day with a big, "GOOD morning." He was clean, pressed, loud, energetic, and perky at a time when everyone else was trying to catch a power nap. And then, all day long, he followed people around and told them what they were doing wrong. The highlight of my summer was the day he took me aside and gave me a fatherly little speech about how, someday, if I kept my nose to the grindstone, all this could be mine. It would be like being the warden on one of those prison planets.

Anyhow, Earl was just too pushy and too nosey to confine his antics to his own little slice of paradise. One day, as I was plodding back to the paint room with something from the mailroom, I witnessed old Earl walk up to a painter on the line, tap him on the shoulder, and offer a bit of unsolicited advice on how the guy could do his job better. The guy climbed down off his ladder REAL slowly, removed his gloves and mask (Earl was still yammering), and, without saying a word, caught Earl on the bridge of the nose with a sweeping overhand right that would have made Ali proud. I thought Earl was dead. He was still out cold when someone threw him on a makeshift stretcher and headed for the hospital. What a day, and me without a camera.

The next week was a treat. Earl came in looking like a greasy-haired Rocky Raccoon, broken nose and eyes all purple and yellow and swollen. His thick safety glasses only served to magnify the problem. For days he snarled and stomped around like a badger with his foot in a trap, and we all dodged him and kept busy. Unfortunately, I don't think he learned anything from his little attitude adjustment (guys like him never do), but I'd have given a week's pay just to see it.

THREE SHEETS TO THE WINDBAG

You've probably heard the phrase, "three sheets to the wind" and figured it had something to do with Amish laundry hanging on the line. Actually, three bed sheets wouldn't make sense. It would have to be two or four, but I digress. Anyhow, the phrase is actually based on sailing lingo. You might logically assume that "sheets" are the sails, but you'd be wrong. Instead, the sheet is the rope or line that controls the trim of the sail and allows it to catch the wind. You're welcome.

Therefore, the phrase refers to what would happen if three lines were loose in the wind at the same time, which would cause the ship to rock drunkenly. Thus, it's slang for a level of inebriation. There are actually four levels, with one being a bit tipsy, and when you hit four, you're comatose on the garage floor.

We were invited to several graduation open houses this summer, and all were very nice with wonderful hosts and delicious food. Most had tea and soft drinks and some had adult beverages. At one of these shindigs, there were fifty or sixty people milling around, eating sandwiches and appetizers and sipping on cold drinks. However, there was one woman, maybe somebody's aunt Betty or a distant cousin or just a party crasher, who skipped the main course and wore a path to the beverage station . . . over and over again.

This wasn't like your typical fraternity party where everybody is drunk and loud and obnoxious and oblivious to the din around them. Instead, it was like having Otis Campbell at a church social. She was three sheets to the wind, working hard on four, and sticking out like a sore thumb (yes, it's classic cliché day).

This made for a very entertaining floor show. She'd slug down another sixteen-ounce beverage, peer through the crowd, select an unsuspecting member of the studio audience, and launch herself into their airspace. I observed that, when you attain level 3.8 on the sheet scale, you become highly intelligent and very philosophical. And, since you have something important to share, it's critical that you lean in as closely as possible to your intended victim's face and regale them with loud and fascinating tidbits gleaned from vast personal experience. A fun little byproduct of this level is a complete lack of awareness that you are simultaneously spitting on their glasses and giving them a personal breathalyzer.

The whole scene reminded me of a Pepé Le Pew cartoon. There was always some poor cat with white paint splashed down her back, and our hero, a suave and debonair French skunk, trying desperately to romance her, while the cat frantically clawed and kicked and tried to escape. This only strengthened Pepé's resolve. In this case, people at that party seemed to suddenly remember some urgent business back home or in Chicago, and hurried off, wiping slobber off their glasses as they went. Unfazed, Aunt Betty just poured another cold one and went off in search of another new best friend.

BAD NEWS

What is it that makes a great comedian better than the rest? It's the delivery. Bob Hope used to stand up in front of thousands of people and tell corny C+ jokes that any of us could have told, and yet somehow he made us all laugh. Similarly, the proper delivery of bad news is a very special talent.

I was sitting in the waiting room of the car repair place a couple weeks ago, crunching on those vending machine Hot Tamales, reading some old *Field & Stream* from 1986, and listening to the guy at the front desk while he called people on the phone to give them the bad news about their vehicles.

It occurred to me that what he was doing was very much like the awful task a surgeon has when he emerges from the operating room to tell some distraught family members the news about a patient. "Mrs. Johnson, I'm very sorry, but he's going to have to remain hospitalized for a few weeks. We accidentally removed his right kidney instead of his appendix. Sorry. Could've happened to anybody."

Anyhow, the guy I was listening to was terrific . . . fast and to the point. In fact, he could actually make you feel good about a several-hundred-dollar repair bill. "Hello, Mr. Wilson? This is Bill down at Barney's Muffler and Pizzeria. Yeah, the good news is that your muffler is fine, but you still need front pads and rear rotors, for a total of $202.47, including tax." The customer never had a chance to flinch. Contrast this with a call I got a while back . . . the verbal equivalent of walking ever so slowly into an ice-cold lake. The conversation went something like this:

Joe: "Hello, Mr. Eastley? Yeah, this is Joe down at Larry's Auto Repair."

Me: "Hi, Joe. What's up? Do you have the scoop on my car?"

Joe: "Yeah, I'm afraid it's bad news, Mr. Eastley."

Me: (stressing out) "What is it, Joe?"

Joe: (thirty seconds of dead silence on the phone)

Me: (B.P. over 200) "Joe, are you there?"

Joe: "Uh . . . I'm afraid you need new front ball joints."

Me: "Oh, that doesn't sound so bad. What are we talking?"

Joe: "Well, those are $400, but you also need rear pads and rotors."

Me: (starting to sweat) "Wow, so how much are we up to?"

Joe: "Well, those are $350."

Me: "Man I was hoping not to drop that much cash, but I guess I have no choice."

Joe: "Uh, well, I'm sorry, but there's more. It looks like you need a new transmission."

Me: (Pulse now exceeding current body weight): "Are you KID-DING me?"

Joe: "No, Mr. Eastley. And then there's your camshaft . . ."

This torture by phone went on for about twenty minutes while I agonized and squirmed and waited for the dreaded bottom line. Next time, here's how I'd rather get the call:

"Hello, Mr. Eastley? This is Joe down at the shop. I'm sorry, but it's bad news. The car is pretty well shot. It needs new shocks-struts-brakes-transmission-main seal-master cylinder-transmission-cam shaft-and electronic ignition system."

"Huh, you mean . . . ?"

"Yes, Mr. Eastley, it's toast. For what it's going to run you, it would be cheaper to build you a brand new BMW from the ground up. Have a nice day."

So, to all of you out there who have to be the bearers of bad news, I have a suggestion. Don't trickle it out at glacier speed. It only makes it worse. Instead, have three or four cups of coffee, take a deep breath, and rip off the Band-Aid.

SEE YOU MAÑANA

Most of us can be lumped into one of two basic personality categories. My old buddy (we'll call him Joe) lives in the U.P. He's definitely Type B. If the guy were any more laid back, he'd be unconscious. I remember when he built his house. He reached the point where it had four walls and a roof, and that was good enough. I've seen rustic campsites with more amenities. The kitchen had a sink with running water, and, in lieu of a pantry, six or eight cardboard boxes full of food and utensils and assorted junk. The cupboards were in, but they had no doors and were covered with rags and old dish towels. The floor was plywood, and there was talk of buying carpet at some nonspecific point in the future. There were no interior doors anywhere in the house. Every doorway was draped with an old curtain. This was seven years after he moved in. No, really.

I lean toward Type A. I might procrastinate for a while about painting the house or some other project, but once I start, I pretty much go full-throttle until it's done. If I'm building a new deck, people have to bring sandwiches and cold drinks out to me and remind me to eat. If I'm driving from here to Colorado, I want to be there NOW. So, I get in the car here, put the pedal down, stop as little as possible, and get out of the car there. Maybe this makes me Type-T (for tunnel-vision), but the thought of lollygagging (I like that word) across the Great Plains on a three or four-day cruise makes me crazy. So do people who drive forty-five mph in the left lane.

Jimmy Buffet wrote the lyrics, "Please don't say mañana if you don't mean it." I always thought "mañana" meant "tomorrow." However, it's not that specific. Just like Joe's alleged carpet installation, it actually refers to "an indefinite point of time in the future."

My good friend Gary was just in town for a visit, and apparently shares my Type-T personality and lack of patience in certain situations. He's a musician who, a few years back, spent some time in Ireland. I may have the details muddled a bit, but he told me of trying to organize some paying gigs in several pubs, and becoming frustrated when the locals kept suggesting that he come back tomorrow or Thursday or maybe next week.

Anyhow, after making several fruitless contacts and becoming totally exasperated, he found himself swilling warm Guinness next to an old man in one of the local taverns. Gary's from Arizona, where there's a significant Hispanic population, and he asked the guy if there's an Irish word comparable to "mañana." The old man smiled and said, "We don't have a word that conveys that level of urgency."

To further illustrate this point, there's a popular theory in those parts that if the Irish had settled in the Netherlands, they'd have drowned. I suppose it would have been immortalized in the very short and tragic story of Sean Brinker, the boy who said he'd get around to plugging that dike "mañana."

A little note to you all you Type B's out there: The world is a nicer place because you are in it, and I envy your 105/70 blood-pressure readings, but please slide into the right lane and get the heck out of my way.

TO MAKE A SHORT STORY LONG . . .

I don't know what it is about some people that renders them incapable of getting to the point. Perhaps it's some recessive gene gone amok (I like that word), or having been exposed to too many Gabby Hayes movies as an infant, or maybe their parents never explained the whole "orifice ratio" concept to them (two ears, one mouth: use proportionally). Regardless, I always seem to get cornered by someone with a long story and too much stamina right when I've got something important to do.

The last time it happened, I was picking up a few groceries at one of our local supermarkets when I ran into an old acquaintance (we'll call him Carl). I was trying to get the goods in record time and zip home in time for a football game, but it wasn't in the cards. Carl had recently taken a trip to Germany or Hawaii or someplace with a group of friends, and he felt compelled to fill me in on the details . . . ALL the details.

The problem with Carl is that, whenever he tells a story, he feels it's important to set the stage and start at the beginning, the VERY beginning. So, I heard (again) about his early years growing up in a log cabin, and walking five miles uphill through the snow each way to school, and how his upbringing was positively influenced by his sixth grade gym coach, and when he was thirteen he had to get braces, and on and on. To make a long story even longer, Carl finds it a little hard to stay focused and frequently gets off on tangents. If he's telling you about last night's hockey game, it'll remind him that he had a slice of pizza between periods, and he'll launch into a massive oration about where you can find the best pizza in Chicago or Detroit or Venice, and it's twenty minutes before he gets back to the game.

So . . . he followed me, talking . . . and talking . . . and talking, up and down every aisle, with me occasionally nodding and saying something witty like, "uh huh," then continued chatting while the checkout girl raised her eyebrows and I paid for the stuff (I think I wrote, "Help Me!" on the check). He even tagged along as I sprinted for the car, oblivious to the fact that I was trying to escape. The worst part was that by the time we'd spent the past thirty minutes together, and I'd finally gotten the groceries loaded, he and his friends hadn't even made it to the airport yet. I spent the next five minutes trying to interject, "Uh, Carl, I really have to ..."blah, blah, blah, "Listen, I'm a little tight for ..." blah, blah, blah, "Really, I'm late for ..."blah, blah, blah, until I finally just rudely turned my back on him, got in the car and drove away. I suspect the guy talks in his sleep.

This is not an isolated case. I like to watch the news and get the latest weather report. Why does it take fifteen minutes for some guys (usually the rookies) to deliver a weather forecast? All I want to hear is, "Cloudy tonight with a thirty percent chance of snow . . . Partly sunny on Friday with a twenty percent chance of rain late in the day. . . and the weekend looks cold and snowy." How long did that take? Ten seconds? Instead, we have to wait and wait and wait while he explains warm fronts and cold fronts and low-pressure systems and Alberta Clippers and jet streams, and waves his arms in front of the national weather map, then finally prognosticates tomorrow's weather, pauses, and says, "in other words . . .", and then goes back over the exact same thing for a second time. Please, I just want to know if I'll be shoveling in the morning.

Alright, we've identified the problem, but what do you do when a longwinded someone drops in or calls you on the phone, and there seems to be no way out? I have some suggestions. These need to be co-ordinated ahead of time. If the person is on the phone, use the doorbell method. You simply hold up the receiver, ring your own doorbell, and say, "Oh, I gotta go . . . someone's at the door." If it's a drop-in visitor, you need to give your spouse a prearranged signal (like you're choking), whereat she slips out of the room, calls the home phone from your cell, and you feign an emergency ("Really? Okay, I'll be right there . . ."). If you're out in public, traveling incognito might just save you an hour. So, if you're at the grocery store and see some idiot wearing rubber glasses, nose, and a mustache, it's probably me.

HRD (HIRE THE REALLY DIMWITTED) TALES

I was both lucky and unlucky enough to have worked for two bosses who hired female help based mostly on their looks. When I was seventeen, I was one of three cooks in a pretty nice family restaurant, and the owner was a rich, dirty old man. I couldn't have been more pleased. My days were spent grilling steaks and flapping flipjacks for seven or eight waitresses who looked like they'd stepped out of a Victoria's Secret catalog, except that they were actually wearing clothes. So, I was happy to volunteer for all the hours I could get. The owner was always coming in and putting his hands on their shoulders or trying to brush up against them, but they just ignored the old geezer and raked in the tips.

Years later, with a different perspective on the "looks versus competency" issue, I was working at an engineering firm for a guy who had absolutely NO concept of the qualities needed in an employee. He obviously didn't grasp the fact that when you hire the wrong person, you're stuck with them until you get a divorce. Anyhow, we needed a new secretary, and he hired the first person that walked in. To say she was a little dim would be like saying Ted Bundy was a little misguided. She couldn't type, couldn't figure out how to transfer phone calls (and thus was constantly hanging up on people), and had this shrill, reedy voice that made you wonder how you were going to make it to five o'clock without sticking an ice pick in your head. She was always on the phone with one of her many family members, or on her CB radio with some of her buddies, and answering every question with "10-4." A typical conversation went like this:

"Are you going to the bar tonight?"

"10-4"

"Is John going with you?"

"10-4"

"What time are you going?"

"10:04"

etc. etc. etc.

I asked her once if it was against the law to say, "Yes" on a CB radio, and she gave me this blank look like I'd asked her to recite the first law of thermodynamics. Anyhow, her crowning achievement occurred when she had to send sets of design drawings to several contractors who wanted to bid on them. She ran off all the copies, stapled them together, and then sent a dozen copies of page one to the first contractor, a dozen of page two to the second contractor, etc. After about the tenth irate phone call to the boss, she was offered the opportunity to find a new line of work. I was thinking that, since she already had that CB thing down, maybe she should drive a big rig. 10-Roger, over and out.

With a void to fill, my boss again did what he did best, and hired the next first person that walked in off the street. She fell into the "cute, but not too bright" category, but she got the job. Just as a full house beats three of a kind, it turns out that an attractive figure beats sub-par office skills. Actually, her work was somewhat adequate, except that she couldn't spell, and this was before computers. She made up for it by entertaining us with a repertoire of carefully crafted idiocies. These were normally blurted out in the lunchroom, where she was the only female in the company of seven or eight men. One time, while downing a bag of potato chips, she noticed one of the guys also crunching away, and said, "My Lays are fifty cents . . . .how much are yours?" It got real quiet. A couple weeks later she reached into a bag, pulled out a sugar doughnut, took a big bite, and with a mouthful of powdered sugar, announced, "I'm giving up sweets." Everyone started chuckling, and she said, "Whaaaa? . . . you know, candy bars and cookies and stuff." Years later, I heard she got married and was on her way to four or five kids. With luck, all they inherited were her looks.

THE WINE IS FINE

I'm a wine kinda sewer. I only like red. I even drink it with fish. Call me a hack, a loser, a subhuman primate . . . I don't care. You can try to convert me with a $200 bottle of Chablis, but it will be a waste of time and money. I don't care much for white, and I can't distinguish the pricy stuff from a ten-dollar bottle.

That brings us to today's topic: true confessions. My cousin (we'll call him Nick) wants to get something off his chest. I offered to help by putting it in writing and sharing it with the twenty-plus people who were present for the event. I only hope the statute of limitations has run out on this one.

Nick has a really old, cool cottage with a Michigan basement (aka hole in the ground) on a lake not far from here. Our family cottage is right next door. There are more cousins in a quarter-mile stretch than you'll find in a Kentucky county.

Anyhow, my brother Mark invited the whole gaggle for an evening of food and merriment. The theme was a 50s party. Nick not only wore a ducktail and dressed in 50s motif, but he brought a bottle of red wine dated 1955, in honor of the year that Mark was born. Party on, 50-something Garth.

He also brought a rather eloquent story about how he had procured such a rare offering. He'd been poking around in the dark recesses of that dank basement and had discovered an old wine reserve stashed there by his father. There had been whispers and rumors about its existence and whereabouts, but everyone just assumed it was folklore. Not anymore.

The bottle itself was very impressive. It was covered with over 50 years of grime, but you could still (barely) make out that ancient date. Everyone marveled. Naturally, there was some concern about the quality of the fermented spirits inside, and whether they had turned to vinegar or something even nastier. There was only one way to find out.

With the greatest of care, Nick opened the bottle and poured a modest splash into each of the twenty or so wine glasses arranged on the table. Every partygoer got a taste, and that taste was, in a word, extraordinary. It was so smooth and flavorful, and everyone agreed that they'd shared a once-in-a-lifetime experience.

I, like the rest of the lemmings and their second lemmings once removed, was yammering on about how this was the finest wine ever enjoyed by human beings when I looked over at Nick and caught just the hint of a smirk and a twinkle in his eye. Hmmm. I discretely took him aside and asked what I'd missed. He whispered that I should take a closer look at the bottle and see if I noticed anything unusual. Well, there it was . . . the ace hidden up his sleeve. Barely visible under that layer of caked-on dirt was . . . drum roll please . . . a bar code.

Talk about your classic illusions. He'd purchased a twelve-dollar bottle of wine from some local grocery store, slathered it with wet clay from the road by the cottage, changed the date with a Sharpie, and concocted (I like that word) this rather elaborate fairy tale. It was genius. And, under the category of "no harm, no foul," everyone left happy and anxious for another party and a second chance to sample more magic elixir from the cottage catacombs (I like that word, too).

Well, now you know. It's not that Nick is plagued with guilt or losing sleep over this little charade. On the contrary, it's just that something this clever is way too much fun to keep, uh, bottled up forever.

REALLY, I'M ME

It seems as though we've gone a little bit, or perhaps a WAY bit overboard trying to protect ourselves from identity theft. Yes, I get it. Bad people want to run up charges on our credit cards or steal our hard-earned dollars out of ATM's or whatever. It's actually why I pay cash and don't even have an ATM card.

Anyhow, do we really need to be so overly protective if a person just wants to pay a bill? Honestly, if one of you nice folks cares to waltz into the gas company and shell out a couple hundred clams to pay my January heating bill, have at it. No, really.

I bring this up because I went to the office of my cell phone provider the other day to pay my bill . . . in cash. Usually, when I walk into a business holding a stack of universal redemption certificates (five of them with pictures of President Jackson on them), I'm greeted rather warmly. Often, I instantly become the new best friend of some young salesman who hopes to take them off my hands in return for something he has on the shelf. Not so in this case. The conversation went something like this:

OCD Salesman: "Hello, sir, is there something I can help you with?"

Local College Professor: "Yes, I'd like to pay my bill."

OCDS: "Will that be cash or credit card?"

LCP (proudly waving $100 to indicate his sincerity) "That'll be cash."

OCDS: "Okay, I'll need to see your driver's license."

LCP: "Really? What for?"

OCDS: "I'm sorry sir. That's our policy."

LCP: "But if I mailed you a check, you wouldn't need to see my license."

OCDS: "I'm sorry sir. That's our policy. Before I can access your account, I have to scan your license. Please initial here indicating that you understand the policy and have authorized us to scan your driver's license."

Somewhat annoyed LCP: "I'm not asking for an account number. I just want to pay the bill. Look (more waving), I have money."

Relentless OCDS: "I'm sorry sir, but that's our policy."

LCP: "Fine, I'll initial it. Now, how much is the bill?"

ROCDS: "I'm sorry sir, but first I have to ask you a few verification questions."

Seriously annoyed LCP: "Verifying what? I don't understand. You just verified my identity by scanning my driver's license. That mug shot looks just like me. All I want to do is pay my bill."

ROCDS: "I'm sorry sir. That's our policy."

LCP (unaware of a slight involuntary tic): "Fine, what do you want to know?"

Name of your elementary school? West.

Mother's maiden name? Wright.

Dog's middle name? Fido.

The square root of 3? 1.732. What does that have to do with paying my bill?

Sir, just a few more questions. Who starred in *Captain Ron*?

I think it was Kurt Russell.

How many doughnuts in a baker's dozen?

Uh, thirteen. Is that it?

No, sir, you need to drop and give me twenty.

Really? These are my good pants.

I'm sorry sir. That's our policy.

Fine, whatever.

ROCDS: "Thank you for your patience."

LCP (twitching like Herbert Lom in *The Pink Panther*): "Does this mean I can finally pay my bill?"

ROCDS: "Well, there is one more small thing. Bring me the broomstick of the Wicked Witch of the West."

CHAPTER 7

MISS ELAINEOUS

FINDING LAS VEGAS

For those of you seeking a vacation destination, I may have found the best-kept secret in the West. It's a nice, quiet little town called Las Vegas, a serene little spot tucked away in the heart of the Nevada desert. In time, I think the place will probably catch on, but right now the only ones who know about it are my wife and myself and perhaps five or six million other people.

In the middle of this little Podunk, they have a road nicknamed "The Strip," which reminds me somewhat of 28th Street in Grand Rapids . . . on lots and lots of caffeine. However, the businesses along this street weren't anything like I expected or even recognized. You can't find a grocery store or a sporting goods shop or even a decent bakery anywhere. Instead, Las Vegas has an inordinately large number of establishments known as "casinos."

As far as I can tell, these casinos are some sort of newfangled restaurant. They have a bunch of very nice and attractive waitresses who come around and offer you all the adult beverages you can drink. Most of them are wearing outfits that may have fit when they were twelve. However, these women aren't in charge of serving food. If you're hungry, they have hundreds and hundreds of these fancy looking coin-operated vending machines. Frankly, I'm surprised people don't starve to death out there. I put money into several of these contraptions and pulled the levers, but never once got a ham sandwich or a Snickers bar or even a bag of Fritos. The guy next to me must have had a defective machine because the light began flashing and it started spitting out more quarters than he could carry, but he never got a candy bar, either.

One evening, I went out for a walk and discovered what a friendly town Las Vegas really is. On every street corner, there were two or three young men very eager to hand me what I thought were baseball cards. As it turns out, each one has a picture of a pretty girl on it and a phone number where she can be reached. They call it an "escort service." I suppose you'd call one of these girls if you were new in town and needed help finding directions, or perhaps if you were an elderly person who needed to be helped across the street. Anyway, I thought it was pretty darn neighborly that these girls were willing to give up their whole Friday evening just to make sure our stay was a pleasant one. The pictures I saw must have been taken on a rather warm day because those girls sure weren't wearing much.

Before you travel out there, you'd be well advised to brush up on some of the local rules and regulations just to be sure you stay out of trouble. Based on what I saw, it's just fine with them if you want to swagger (or stagger) down the street carrying a two-foot-high margarita, wearing nothing but a thong, hollering obscenities at the moon, and offering to sell your body parts to anyone who'd have them. But . . . if you even THINK about venturing out into an intersection against a "Don't Walk" sign, you'll find yourself up to your ears in local law enforcement.

So, if you're headed out there, have a ball. Don't forget your thong and some sweatshirts for the escort girls, and maybe a Roger Maris or Mike Trout to trade with the guys on the corner. Oh, yeah, and maybe bring along a box of granola bars, just in case those vending machines still haven't been fixed.

I'VE BEEN CANNED

My father-in-law, who grew up on a farm, said they never had much money, but they always had plenty to eat. They canned meat, vegetables, eggs, fruit, and pretty much anything that wasn't tied down. His favorite line was, "We'll eat what we can, and what we can't eat, we'll can." Words to live by.

I have copious can issues in my garage. The problem is that I own a lawn mower, a snow blower, a chainsaw, a weed whacker, an outboard motor, two backpack leaf blowers, and several other gas-guzzling, ozone-dissolving gizmos. The associated issue is that some of these use gasoline only, while the rest require a gas/oil mixture, each with its own 50:1 or 40:1 or 35:1 or some other blend requiring a Ph.D. in metric conversions, with absolutely no two being the same. Therefore, you need a separate gas can for each smelly toy in the garage.

Exacerbating the problem is the fact that I have one or two previous generations of these motorized monsters lying about in various stages of disintegration or disassembly, and each one of them also has its own gas can. "So," you say, being logical and practical, "why not just get rid of them?" Well, that's easier said than done. Have you ever tried throwing out old containers holding flammable liquid? I have various and sundry gas cans in my garage, each half-full of old, unusable gasoline. I can't ditch the stuff out back without poisoning my groundwater. The dump doesn't want them. The trash removal service won't take them. My only choice is to move. The term "various and sundry" is actually a redundant phrase, which makes it perfect for describing the myriad (I like that word) of redundant red cans lying about in my container graveyard.

There was a time when I had this mess pretty well under control. I think Reagan was president at the time. Each gas can had a label on it in magic marker along with its mix ratio. It said something like,

"Husqvarna, 40:1." Since then, each can has accumulated a quarter inch of dust, the black marker has faded to a light gray, and I can no longer tell them apart. It's quite a conundrum, or perhaps I should say, a CANundrum.

I would also like to voice a complaint about the cause of this whole dilemma. Why is every motor different? Why can't they all just be 50:1, and we feed them all from one big can? Furthermore, have you seen the containers the mixing oil comes in? They're purchased in some convenient size like eight ounces or sixteen ounces, but of course, you need 3.33 ounces.

You can wing the first batch, but after that, the partially full oil bottle has between nine and ten ounces in it, and you need 4.25 ounces., so you have to rush in and study fractions before you can even think about cutting wood. That's IF you can read the oil level through that opaque side slot, which I find next to impossible. Finally, frustrated, you pour some random amount of oil into the gas can and hope you're somewhere in the ballpark.

So, here's your assignment for next time. You have a weed whacker requiring gasoline with 2.75 ounces of oil per gallon. Your gas can holds 1.75 gallons of gas. Your oil bottle currently has 8.5 ounces of oil in it. So, the obvious question is, how can you sneak out to the golf course without your wife noticing?

SPRING BREAK: GLACIERS GONE WILD

Our little planet seems to have a big old bulls-eye painted on it. Over sixty million years ago (give or take a month) we had dinosaurs wandering around in blissful ignorance, oblivious to the fact that the sky was about to fall. That's when, according to one theory, a meteor about six miles in diameter doing 40,000 mph collided with earth down on the Yucatan Peninsula. They called it a Cretaceous-Tertiary extinction event. That's scientific jargon for "the dinosaur droppings hit the fan." It threw the planet into total darkness, caused wildfires, earthquakes and volcanoes, and barbequed a bunch of Brontosauri.

Our next cataclysmic event is happening a bit more slowly, but the results are equally frightening. Yes, we're talking global warming. The ice caps are dwindling, the polar bears can't find a place to hunt for seals, and all that melting ice is raising sea levels. And, as we've all heard, the major cause is allegedly greenhouse gas emissions, but there is another theory that scientists haven't yet considered.

Yes, this next great calamity befalling our planet is being caused by . . . drum roll please . . . spring break. No, really. It's happening right now. In 2010, there were 20.3 million college students in the United States. Let's assume an average weight of 150 pounds each, and conservatively say that half of them head south for a week of sun and fun and alcoholic debauchery. Since there are fractions and long division involved, I'll spare you the math. Just take my word for it that 750,000 tons of student body are presently descending on a very small area of Florida and Mexico all at the same time.

The result of this is much like that asteroid strike. The sudden, concentrated shifting of weight on the earth's surface causes it to rotate in a counterclockwise direction. People think global warming is a recent phenomenon. Actually, this has been going on since 1965, when every teenager in America saw *Beach Blanket Bingo* and just HAD to go looking for Annette and Frankie.

As a result, the North Pole, previously frigid and unforgiving, has been migrating south for over fifty years and is currently in the spatial coordinates originally occupied by Dubuque, Iowa. Meanwhile, Dubuque has moved on to Houston, and well, you get the picture.

Anyhow, as this big shift occurs, the polar ice cap is now more exposed to the direct rays of the sun, causing accelerated glacial melting. The water sloshes south, raising ocean levels by several inches, and its tsunami effect generally makes for excellent surfing. This is hugely appealing to all those half-naked college students baking in the sun in places like Daytona and Ft. Lauderdale. So, the next year, heeding the cry of "surf's up," even more students head for the beach, and the world shifts even more. It's an ongoing cycle.

Unfortunately, this is likely to continue for another hundred years or so. At that point, we'll have experienced a full 180-degree inversion, the South Pole will be relocated where the North Pole used to be, and we'll have penguins living at the top of the world. The downside is that those of us from Michigan and Minnesota will start speaking with an Australian accent, and Santa's GPS will be totally discombobulated (I really like that word, mostly because it has a "bob" in it). Well, at least the polar ice caps will stop melting. I just thought you should know.

FOLLOW THE LITER

A number of you have written and asked me to explain the nuances of the metric system, just on the odd chance that we're invaded and conquered by Canada. Okay, I made that up. Nobody wrote to me. I just knew that, secretly, you were yearning for learning about metrics.

Historically, I believe the first major dimensional snafu occurred when God told Noah to build an ark that was 300 cubits by fifty cubits by thirty cubits. While Noah was a great man who lived to be 950 years old and was renowned both for his preaching and for discovering the soothing effects of wine (no, really), he wasn't much of a builder. In short, he didn't know a cubit from a camel.

To make matters worse, there's a twenty-inch standard cubit, which measures from the elbow to the tip of the middle finger, and also a lower forearm cubit, which is only twelve inches from the elbow to the hand, so it was all very confusing. In the end, he just built it in meters, which is why his oversized houseboat ended up larger than the *USS Yorktown*. No wonder his neighbors were snickering.

Years ago, the State Highway Department in Michigan actually started producing all their construction blueprints in metric units. I guess they figured we should become more global and follow the rest of the lemmings. I'm surprised that the contractors weren't required to submit bids in euros. Anyhow, just like Noah, these contractors had trouble converting from meters to feet (I think you multiply by 2.54, add the national debt, and divide by your IQ). Anyhow, the whole thing fizzled, which is good, because otherwise, your odometer would be counting kilometers.

Therefore, in an effort to provide continuing education and contribute to the common good, allow me to offer the following definitions for certain metric terms. You can thank me later.

Liter: The head of a country or state. See Vladimir Putin.

Meter: A bottomless coin-eating slot machine which sits atop a steel post and demands a dollar donation for thirty minutes of parking.

Millimeter: A tiny version of the device described above for today's newfangled midget electric cars.

Gram: A cracker often eaten by second-graders, usually with milk. Also, the dry, boring component of S'mores that keeps the good stuff from escaping.

Newton: Cake-like cookies filled with figs or raspberries or other gooey fruit. They were invented by some guy named Isaac.

Watt: A type of inquiry often used when responding to a spouse. For example, "Honey, did you take out the garbage?" . . . long pause . . . "Watt?" See also, "Huh?"

Joules: Also known as "bling," it includes diamonds, rubies, and other precious stones, worn ostentatiously (I love that word) for the purpose of irritating one's peers.

Scaramucci: A unit of time, generally considered to be ten days or 240 hours. The number is identical in both the English and the metric systems of units.

I hope this helps. In parting, here's a little quiz for next time: How many Scaramuccis did it take to finish a keg of wine on the ark?

HAS YOUR WARDROBE MALFUNCTIONED?

You probably remember Super Bowl XXXVIII when Justin Timberlake (1.0) reached over, and with an allegedly unrehearsed flick of the wrist caused Janet Jackson's wardrobe to malfunction. These are the idiots who put the XXX in 38. Anyhow, a portion of her anatomy (if you enjoy eating chicken, it wasn't the thigh or leg) popped right out, and she, of course, was flabbergasted (I love that word). The garment in question appeared to have been spring-loaded, like a mousetrap in reverse, and their little stunt amounted to the musical version of Bullwinkle pulling a rabbit out of a hat.

On the other end of the clothing spectrum is formal or semi-formal attire. You know . . . the monkey suit you had to wear to your grandparents' house for holiday dinners. My department recently hosted one of those year-end events where everyone shows up in sport coats and pantsuits (no, Hilary wasn't there) for a day of meetings and merriment. Gosh, there's nothing I like better than wearing a three-piece suit with a tourniquet cinched around my neck, looking like an extra from an old Bogart movie, but I digress.

Late that day, one of our student office workers brought something to my attention that I'd never considered. Ashley said, "Why do they put so many &#@%*$# hooks and buttons on dress clothes?" Hmmmmm . . . Why, indeed?

This particular young lady is a self-proclaimed procas— . . ., proclas—. . ., uh, person who puts off doing things until the last minute. Apparently, this becomes an issue if you just gulped down three iced teas and really, really, really need to go.

So, as she described it, she was in the ladies' room, knees clamped together, scant seconds from needing a Depends, and frantically, feverishly, futilely attempting to negotiate an oversized button, two met-al hooks, a jammed zipper, some Velcro thingy, and an ultra-skinny two-pronged belt designed for tiny little fingers. Houdini couldn't have escaped from this thing. In short, it had none of the qualities of Janet Jackson's quick-release slingshot.

My suit pants are likewise equipped with two hooks and three buttons in two places. I'm not sure if they're designed for slimming, or just so they don't blow after one of those big, corporate lunches.

There are two possible solutions. The first is for all of us to start wearing polyester slacks with elastic waistbands and no other connection contraptions (also a good word). The second is to have the 2000s officially declared as a "casual century," and we can wear jeans at all times until 2099. I vote for Plan B.

WRESTLE MANIAC

The other night, as I toggled through the intellectual channels (the Kardashians, *Real Housewives*, etc.), I happened upon *WWE Raw*, or whatever they're calling the critically acclaimed professional wrestling show these days. I watched it just long enough to see two guys, about 320 pounds apiece, with long, greasy hair, and tiny little Speedos that accentuated every, uh, protrusion, taking turns breaking chairs over each other's heads. It was quite realistic, just like The Three Stooges. While this was going on, people, literally hundreds of people, were screaming and yelling as if they were at a sporting event.

So, my only question is . . . Huh?!?!? How can this still be happening? That is, we now have cage fighting, where real gladiators with cauliflower ears and their noses on sideways beat each other to a bloody pulp. No Speedos . . . no chairs . . . just pain and bruises. How can it be that professional wrestling hasn't suffered the same fate as the Edsel and the monochrome monitor? I can only assume that the same people rooting for their favorite wrestlers got lost trying to keep up with the

Kardashians and accidentally wandered into the WWE venue.

Not only that but what happened to all those great wrestlers from the days of yore? I can remember, back when I believed in the Easter Bunny and the Tooth Fairy and the thing in the closet, that I also thought pro wrestling was real. They had cool, scary names like Andre the Giant, Abdullah the Butcher, The Crusher, The Sheik, and Strangler Lewis. So, I looked up some of today's most popular chair throwers, and (in addition to Bobby Knight) they have names like Chris Benoit, Shawn Michaels, and Bill Goldberg. Gosh, my heart goes into palpitations at the mere mention!

Anyhow, I'm thinking that if professional wrestling wants to stay afloat, they really need to sound nastier and more intimidating. One strategy would be to borrow from a list of serial killers and give them all three names. Remember John Wayne Gacy and Henry Lee Lucas? Or, simply give them monikers (I like that word) that remind us of today's scariest people.

You probably have your own ideas, but I have a few suggestions. How about "Nasty" Nancy Grace? Then there's "Hawkeye" Dick Cheney and Sam "The Suer" Bernstein. For those of us who attended Michigan Tech a few decades back, I'd offer up Myron "The Chemist" Berry, who struck fear into the hearts of a thousand scared little freshmen every year.

If we want to expand into the international scene and enter the world of grouchy little dictators, there's Kim "The Nuke" Jong-un, and his sidekick, Mahmoud "The Alphabet" Ahmadinejad. That's just off the top of my head, but it beats the heck out of "Bill Goldberg."

YOU TAKE THAT BACK

It's mid-January, and you know what that means. The parties are over, the Christmas trees are by the curb, and you now have to dispose of those five or six presents that need to be relocated. Whether it's a skin-tight blouse designed to show off your middle-aged navel, a nifty new moose call, or a propane-powered cheese grater, you simply don't anticipate a need for it in next fifty years or so.

A friend of mine was lamenting that of the four gifts he bought his wife for Christmas, one was too large, one too small (the Goldilocks syndrome), one a repeat of something he gave her last year, and one just plain ugly. In short, she took them all back and exchanged them. This was further reinforced to me when I was in a clothing store in early January, and there were scads of women in there with boxes and gift receipts returning half the inventory sold the previous month. One poor lady, in particular, was exchanging a rather hairy-looking sweater that was the most dreadful thing I've ever seen. I'm not sure I could accurately describe the color, but if you were to skin an orangutan and sew green patches to its elbows, well, you get the picture.

Allowing men to buy presents for their wives creates problems on several levels. First, ninety percent of their tastes are the exact opposite of what their wives really wear. He'll either come home with a scanty little thing that looked nice on the mannequin at Victoria's Secret, and is suitable only for hookers and anorexic girls under the age of twenty, or he'll get her a new hunting jacket.

Secondly, if he actually goes out shopping and makes an effort to find the perfect gift, there's a mandatory (and uncomfortable) grace period during which she has to pretend to adore it. So, how can you tell if the orangutan sweater you've picked out isn't quite what she had in mind? On Christmas morning, she'll open it up and say, "Oh, I just love it, really!" It could be a burlap sack with paisley accents, and she'd still love it. However, if January 7 or 8 rolls around, and the gift is still in the laundry room, sitting in the box, with the receipt in plain sight, you know its days are numbered. One afternoon, it will simply disappear, and she'll be wearing something new in navy blue.

I suppose it's in the spirit of the holidays if ugly presents get to spend Christmas in a nice home, but let's recap the chain of events.

First, some guy who wears black pants with brown shoes and a blue shirt goes out and buys an article of clothing for his wife at full retail price. It lurks, undetected, in a box under a tree until Christmas morning, at which time it springs out at some poor, unsuspecting recipient. Naturally, she's thrilled. However, after the obligatory two-week holding period, said recipient will suddenly discover that the article has a flaw or doesn't fit quite right, and will suggest that she should exchange it. Unfortunately, she'll discover that there are no other similar garments in her size (since all were procured by her husband's hunting buddies), so she'll be forced to select another clothing item which is not only tasteful but also seventy percent off the pre-holiday price.

In summary (with a few exceptions), the entire male shopping experience is a waste of time. Many hours and dollars are spent just so an ugly sweater can be treated to a long weekend and a round-trip ride in the car. So, I have a proposal. The end result of all this is that your wife waits until the after-Christmas sales are in full swing, and then goes down and picks out exactly what she wants for half-off. Why should you cause her the embarrassment of having to make excuses ("You see, my husband is color blind . . .") and stand in long customer service lines to make returns? Instead, take her out for a nice Christmas brunch, and somewhere around January 7, hand her a roll of hundred-dollar bills and offer to be her shopping chauffeur.

JACK THE RIPPER

Just yesterday, I was trying to start my morning in a healthy way, so I decided on Grape Nuts. Unfortunately, they didn't decide on me. Have you ever tried to open one of their adult-proof containers? Honestly, if you were stuck on a desert island with a case of the stuff, you could starve to death. It's easier to open a coconut with a teaspoon.

The bag inside the box was some sort of indestructible plastic that was born on the planet Krypton. The top was welded shut with what must have been industrial-strength Gorilla Glue. Luckily, I own a chainsaw, or I'd have been eating leftover spaghetti for breakfast.

The incident got me thinking about my dad. His name was Ross, but, like my way-cool grandson, it should have been Jack. Not Sprat or Frost or O'-lantern, but as in Jack the Ripper. When it came to food packaging, my dad was the Terminator. No cereal box or bag of potato chips went unscathed. He left a path of destruction in his wake whenever he went to the pantry.

Let's say you're opening a box of Frosted Flakes. Let's just say. First, you slide your finger under the top flap to break it loose. Then you pop each end of the lower flap free from the end tabs. Finally (at least in the good old days), you gently pull on both sides of the bag to break the seal and pour a big bowl of that GRRRREAT stuff.

Not Jack, er, Ross. You could accurately say that he was wound just a fraction tighter than the average guy. Performing tedious, nitpicky (I like that word) little tasks, such as tying a #18 Ginger Quill, wasn't his forte. In his defense, I'm sure that his original plan was to open that cereal box with all the gentle precision of a brain surgeon. Sure.

However, after accidentally tearing the top flap and slicing his finger open in the process, he resorted to Plan B. That poor, innocent box never had a chance. The resulting carnage reminded me of a tyrannosaurus rex opening a Jeep on *Jurassic Park*. For years, I just assumed that we had a grizzly bear living in the basement.

When you were a kid, did you ever go camping and try to open your pork & beans with the handy-dandy can opener on your Swiss army knife? It usually took about an hour and a half. Since then, the packaged food industry has made huge advances in most of their products. You can buy your tuna in a pouch. There are boxes of chicken broth with screw tops, resealable bags of sliced cheese, and you can now get those canned beans with a handy pull-tab.

However, I see no progress in the cereal industry. If anything, it's gotten worse. And, as it turns out, I apparently favor my dad when it comes to certain personality traits. If the truth be known, there's a traumatized box of Rice Krispies in our pantry right now with a shredded bag and a missing flap. Honestly, it wasn't entirely my fault . . .